Fight on Sioux

FIGHT ON SIOUX, WE'RE ALL FOR YOU

WE'RE THOUSANDS OF STRONG AND LOYAL SOULS

WE KNOW YOU'LL WIN EVERY GAME YOU'RE IN

NO MATTER HOW DISTANT THE GOALS

AS WE GO, WE'LL SHOW EACH FOE THAT

WE'RE THE TOUGHEST TEAM BETWEEN THE POLES

WE'RE ROUGH AND TOUGH IT'S TRUE

BUT WE'RE SPORTSMEN THROUGH AND THROUGH

WE'RE THE FIGHTING SIOUX FROM NORTH DAKOTA U

Bob Peabody, a Sioux goalie from Grand Forks, N.D., who played on UND's 1959 NCAA championship team, played in an era before goalies wore face masks and in a time when the interior of UND's Winter Sports Building could be mighty cold, judging by the cloud from Peabody's breath. (photo, UND Special Collections)

Published by

*Grand Forks (N.D.) Herald,
a Knight Ridder newspaper*

Printed by

*Century Creations Printing, Inc.
Grand Forks, N.D.*

Copyright 2001 by Grand Forks Herald

ISBN 0-9642860-5-X

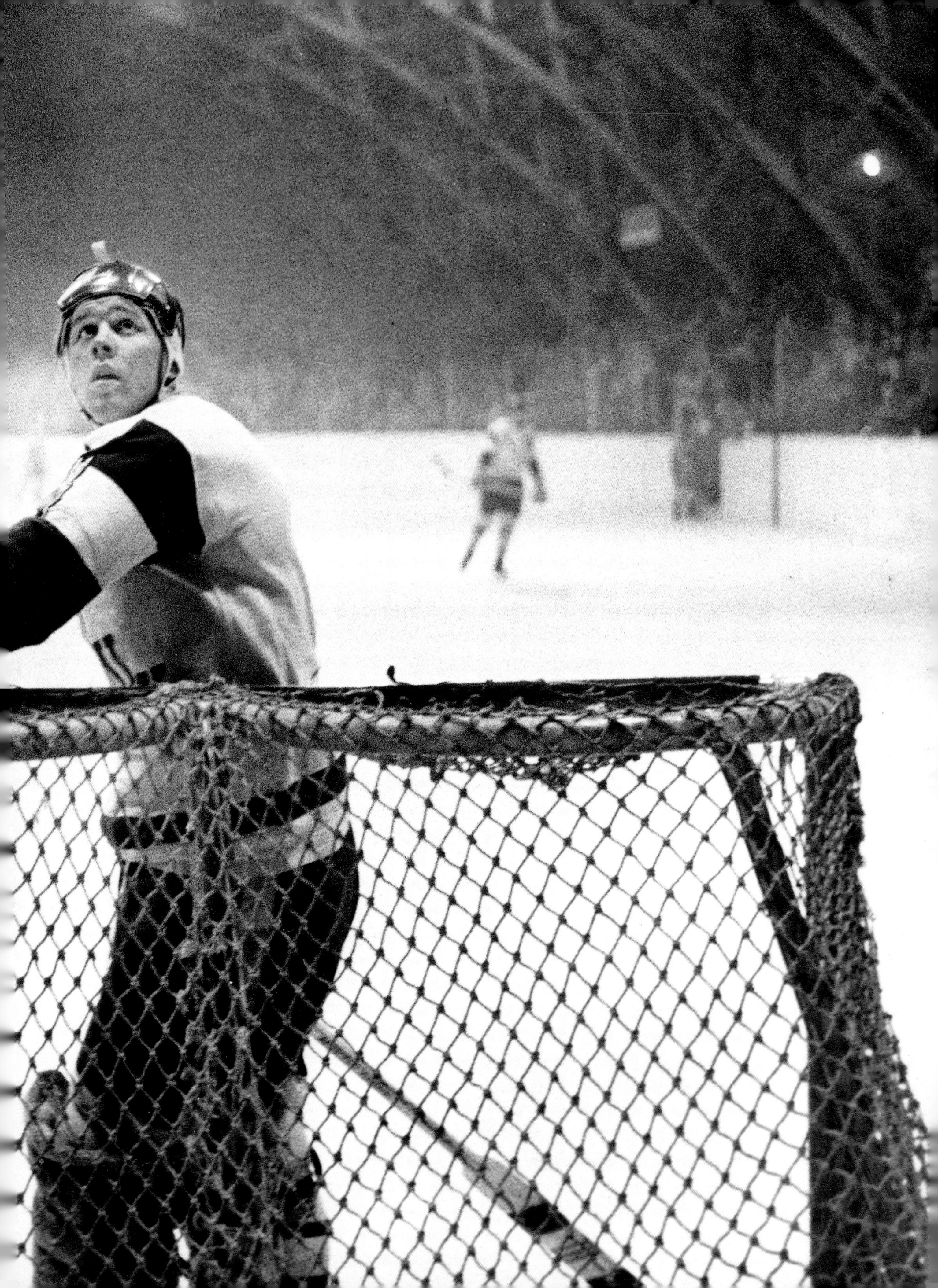

About the writer/*Virg Foss*

No, it's not UND's latest recruit. It's Virg Foss, who has covered Fighting Sioux hockey for 31 seasons and the game of college hockey maybe longer than any sportswriter in the country.

Dedication

To all the players who have worn the Fighting Sioux jersey with such great pride and success; to the coaches who built the program to what it is today, the nation's finest; to the thousands of loyal fans; to former goalie Ralph Engelstad for his gift of the world's finest college hockey rink; to my parents, Maebel Johnson Foss Otteson and the late Rev. Virgil T. Foss, who nourished my passion for sports at an early age and gave me their full support and love in all the years that followed.

— **Virg Foss**

Virg Foss has covered the Western Collegiate Hockey Association longer than any other human in history — since 1969, in fact. A Scobey, Mont., native, he learned hockey on the outdoor rinks in Grand Forks, N.D., in the early 1950s. He was a goalie on the NCAA Division III St. Olaf College teams from 1958 to 1962 in Northfield, Minn.

Foss' claim to fame?

Playing on the St. Olaf freshman team against cross-town rival Carleton College in the 1958-1959 season, he blanked the Carls for half the game. When Carleton's only goalie was injured halfway through the game, the Carleton coach said his team would have to forfeit.

Instead, Foss volunteered to slip on a Carleton jersey so the game could go on.

He blanked his own St. Olaf team the rest of the way. So, he was on the winning side and the losing side all in one game.

He might be the only athlete in NCAA history to play for two colleges in one game.

Grand Forks Herald sportswriter Virg Foss (left) shares a conversation with coach Gino Gasparini in the early 1980s. Foss and Gasparini once were roommates in Grand Fork, N.D. (photo, John Stennes, Grand Forks Herald)

Opposite: *The agony and the ecstasy. Lee Goren celebrates the game-clinching goal as the Sioux beat Boston (Mass.) College 4-2 in the 2000 NCAA title game. As Frozen Four Most Outstanding Player Goren celebrates, Boston's Mike Mottau, who won the Hobey Baker Memorial Award that season, slumps to the ice in Providence, R.I. (photo, Eric Hylden, Grand Forks Herald)*

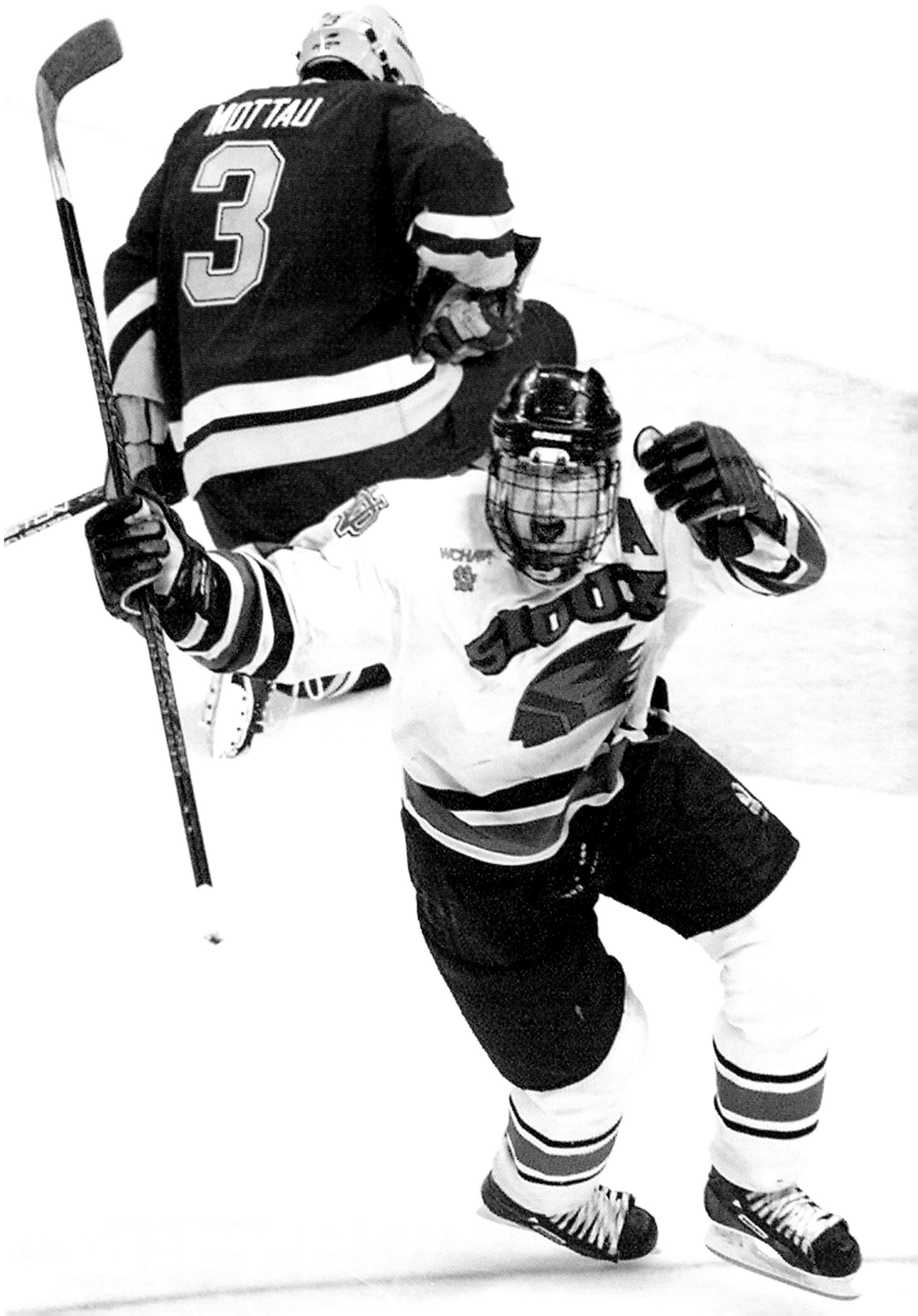
MOTTAU
3
SIOUX
WCHA

Foreward *by Dean Blais*

**"Players have had a
tremendous amount
of success playing
professional hockey
after leaving North
Dakota, but countless
others have achieved
national fame and
recognition in business
and finance."**

Coach Dean Blais

The history of Fighting Sioux hockey is chronologically described by Virg Foss in this book. The many years of winning seasons, championship teams, successful players and coaches and outstanding moments in UND hockey history are described by Foss in a colorful and descriptive way.

No other person in college hockey has the knowledge and ability to recall the experiences and traditions of the Fighting Sioux.

There are more than 50 years of UND hockey, highlighted by seven NCAA championships and 11 Western Collegiate Hockey Association titles.

Players have had a tremendous amount of success playing professional hockey after leaving North Dakota, but countless others have achieved national fame and recognition in business and finance.

Fans who support the team are second to none. Each year, captains from all WCHA teams pick Engelstad Arena as the top place to play with the best atmosphere.

With the new 11,400-seat arena, more fans will get the opportunity to see the Sioux play in college hockey's finest facility.

I hope you enjoy reading about these past teams and players who continue to show unparalleled support to Sioux hockey.

GO SIOUX!

*— Dean Blais,
UND hockey coach*

Opposite: The cup runneth over. At least it does in 1999, when Sioux coach Dean Blais hoists the MacNaughton Cup to celebrate UND's third-straight Western Collegiate Hockey Association title. With the hat trick of titles, UND ties a league record for consecutive MacNaughton Cups won, set from 1994 through 1996 by Colorado College. (Photo, Scott Fredrickson)

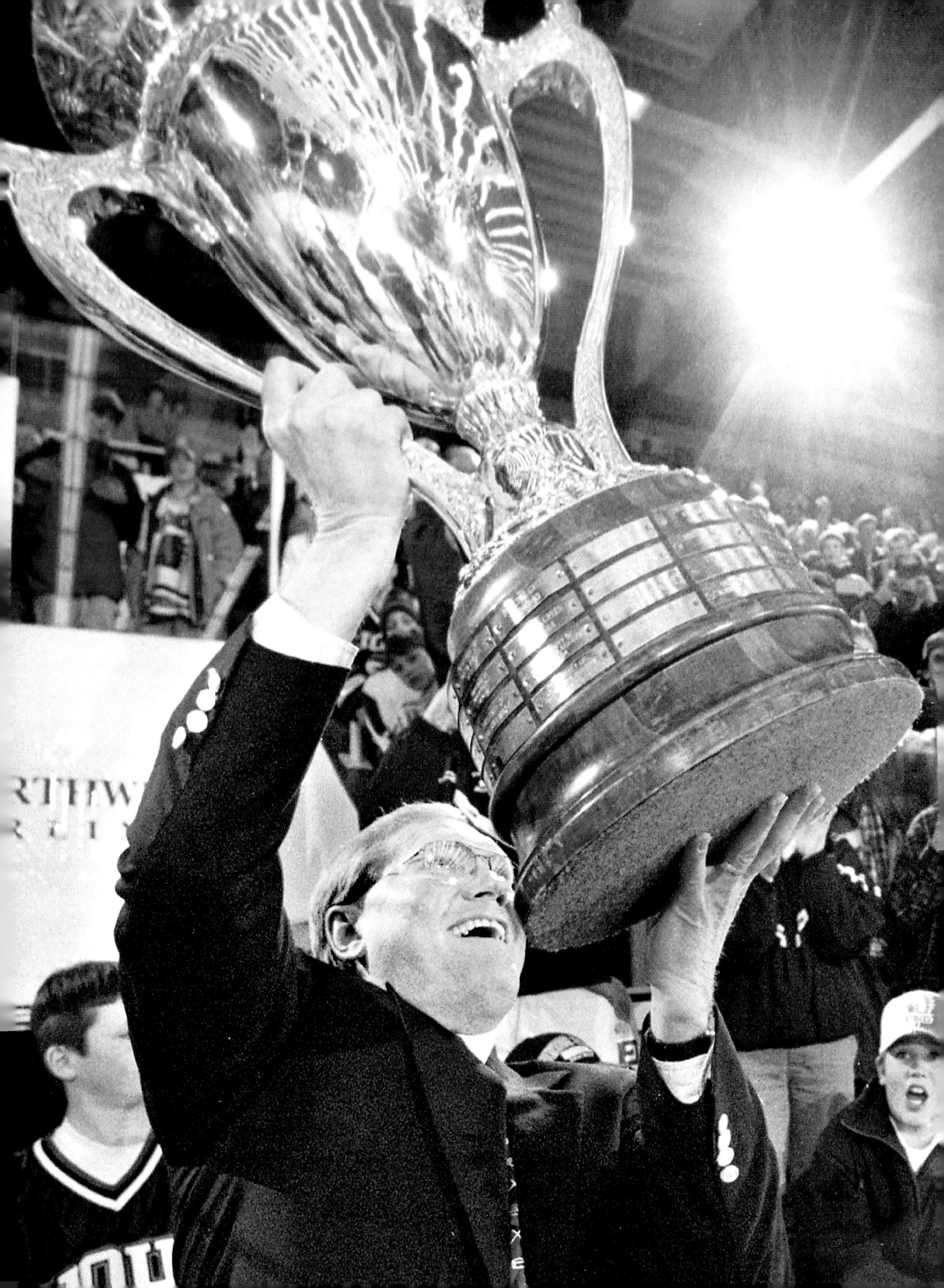

A grinding season of 40 games comes down to this in 1980. In Providence, R.I., the fruits of a 31-8-1 season are celebrated by the Sioux after a 5-2 victory over Northern Michigan in the title game. Even Sioux captain Mark Taylor (back, arm in sling) has reason to smile, despite breaking his collarbone early in the game. (photo, John Stennes, Grand Forks Herald)

Introduction
This is Fighting Sioux hockey

When the upstart University of North Dakota team upset mighty Michigan in Ann Arbor in 1948, it was a victory that later was marked as the official entry into big-time college hockey for the Fighting Sioux.

It would have taken a visionary of extraordinary perception to predict what would happen in the 50-plus years since.

UND's stunning victory over the University of Michigan was a historic moment in Sioux hockey and served as the springboard for a program that now ranks as the nation's finest in terms of staff, facilities and success.

Since 1948, UND's seven national championships are second only to the nine accumulated by Michigan's Wolverines. But six of Michigan's titles came between 1948 and 1956, when college hockey wasn't nearly as widespread and nationally competitive as it is today.

Since UND's first NCAA title in 1959, for example, the Sioux have won seven NCAA crowns compared with three for Michigan.

Yet the history of Sioux hockey is far more than championships, victories and losses. It's about players who have worn the green and white — some 500 of them since 1948 — and fans who follow them with undying passion.

Ralph Engelstad is both. A goalie out of Thief River Falls, Minn., Engelstad first played for the Sioux in 1948. More than half a century later, he repaid his alma mater with the gift of a $100 million arena — the talk of the college hockey world.

UND has done more than win Western Collegiate Hockey Association and NCAA championships. It has turned out many players who moved on to the National Hockey League.

UND was the proving ground for those players. It's where they polished their games and learned discipline under such coaches as John "Gino" Gasparini and Dean Blais and a bevy of excellent assistant coaches.

Diggin' In The Twine

**I'm just dig, dig, diggin'
in the twine,
Dig, dig, diggin' in
the twine.
If you wonder why I wrote
this ditty,
It's because my
defensemen are ------,
So I'm just dig, dig diggin'
in the twine.**

*A poem by Al Finkelstein,
Sioux goalie, 1951-1953*

Not every player to emerge from UND's program made it to the NHL. Some, of course, never played a game of pro hockey at any level. But it's hard to find any who don't retain a great loyalty to UND.

When former Sioux goalie Ed Belfour helped the Dallas Stars win the 1999 Stanley Cup, he brought the storied trophy back to UND that summer for a public celebration. It was his way of saying thanks to the school and its fans.

When the Sioux made it to the 2001 NCAA Frozen Four, Belfour shaved his hair to honor them. And even today, he wears a patch of his old Sioux jersey sewn into his NHL uniform.

There still are a number of UND graduates on pro rosters from coast to coast — and more on their way.

A number of former Sioux also have gone into pro and college hockey in other areas — as coaches, scouts, administrators.

Those players in those roles still play a part in UND's success. They help steer talented players to UND.

Judging by UND's record over the years, they've done a great job.

It's unbelievable what has gone on over the years since UND hockey hit the big time.

The Sioux have a program that is the envy of colleges everywhere.

They now have a rink that cannot be matched by any college — nor by most cities with professional teams.

When UND built the old Winter Sports Center, which opened in 1972, there were those who questioned whether UND could attract enough fans to fill the 6,067 seats.

But once success arrived on campus with the Gino Gasparini era, that problem vanished.

No need to call a taxi. Sioux players give coach Bob May a ride off the ice on their shoulders after UND wins the NCAA championship game on March 14, 1959, in Troy, N.Y. The Sioux defeat Michigan State 4-3. (photo courtesy of Bob May)

In most years since, the Sioux have played to sellout crowds.

There were many more who questioned the sanity of building an 11,400-seat rink, the gift from Engelstad. They'd never sell it out, detractors said.

Wrong again.

Interest in UND's hockey program has resulted in all the seats being sold before the first game. There's even a waiting list for season tickets.

It's the hottest game in town and in the state of North Dakota.

From the days in the unheated "barn" called the Winter Sports Building to the palace on the prairie — the new Ralph Engelstad Arena — it's been quite a ride for Sioux hockey.

And you know what? The journey is just beginning.

About this book

Part of the proceeds from the sale of this book will be donated to the University of North Dakota in Grand Forks. The book was created by Grand Forks Herald staff, who would like to thank the university for sharing its photography archives.

Writer
Virg Foss

Editor
Kevin Fee

Designer/project leader
Janelle Vonasek

Artist/production coordinator
Bobbi DuChamp

Assistant project leader
Matt Cory

Photo collections/statistics
Jenelle Stadstad

Photo editor
Eric Hylden

Photo toning
Lori Weber Menke

Cover designer
Wayne Elfman

Herald managing editor
Kevin Grinde

Herald editor
Mike Jacobs

Concept development
Jim Wall

The photographs in this book are a compilation of Grand Forks Herald photographers — past and present — former Fighting Sioux hockey players, fans and UND's Dakota Student, University Relations, Special Collections and athletic department.

table of contents

Humble beginning

Cal Marvin and his friends talked the University of North Dakota into going big-time Division I in 1948. From humble beginnings to a $100 million rink more than 50 years later, it's been one glorious ride for Sioux hockey. 17

Taste of success

Bob May's team was the first from UND to win a national title. It was a season that began with tragic news from Canada and ended in triumphant news from New York. 22

Revenge: Title No. 2

How sweet it was. After losing the MacNaughton Cup in the WCHA playoffs to Denver (Colo.) University, the Sioux traveled to Chestnut Hill, Mass., to get another shot at the Pioneers in the NCAA title game. This time, the ending was different. 29

All Gino did was win

*John "Gino" Gasparini's
hiring in 1978 and his firing in 1994
both were controversial. But in his
16 years as head coach, Gasparini
brought the Fighting Sioux program
back to national prominence. He also
stocked rosters of NHL
teams with his players.* 35

Inevitable champions

*The 1980 title team was so good, so
skilled, that its coach wondered at
times how it ever lost a game. When
it counted, the Sioux didn't lose.
They ran off 14 straight wins to close
the season with the school's third
NCAA championship — and first
since 1963.* 42

The Wisconsin wars

*Never in college hockey history has
such a collection of talent been
matched in an NCAA championship
game as in Providence, R.I.,
witnessed in 1982. The combined
rosters of UND and Wisconsin had
20 players move on to
play in the NHL.* 51

The Hrkac Circus

*The circus set up camp at UND in
1986-1987. It was actually what
became known nationally as
the Hrkac Circus, led by ringmaster
Tony Hrkac, UND's only
Hobey Baker Memorial
Award winner.* 58

Blais-ing a trail

Longtime assistant coach Dean Blais returned to coaching high school hockey to prepare himself to be a college head coach. When that opportunity came at UND in 1994, he didn't take long to prove himself. **69**

All for one

The 1997 title team always will be remembered as much for the senior goalie who stepped aside as it will for the freshman goalie who led it to the crown. Mighty Michigan was favored to win, but it was the "smurfs" from UND who ruled. **76**

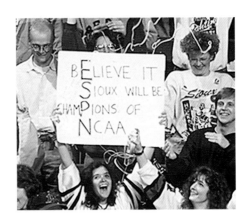

True grit and destiny

Peter Armbrust, Brad DeFauw, Tim O'Connell and Jason Ulmer entered college hockey in 1997 with a bang and left it four years later with the same fireworks. They were key figures on NCAA title teams as both freshmen and seniors, a rare achievement. **87**

Lord of the rinks

From the humble beginnings of the old Winter Sports Building to the state-of-the-art $100 million Ralph Engelstad Arena, UND's three rinks could tell some great stories if they could talk. **97**

Tough guys, tough talk

Has there ever been a player who so terrorized opponents as did Jim Archibald, the NCAA's all-time penalty leader? And how about that brawl in Madison, Wis., in 1982? That's the fight between the Sioux and the Badgers, the one that spilled into the beer garden. 103

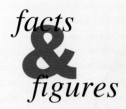

Just a win away

Maybe one more save or one more Sioux goal separated them from being champions. Four times since the NCAA hockey tournament began in 1948, UND teams reached the title game, only to be turned back, often by the slimmest of margins. 112

facts & figures

Turn to page 122 for 22 more pages of pictures, letter-winners, career and season-by-season records, high honors, history and tournament facts.

Home-grown talent

The late Al "Keys" Purpur was a legend as rink manager at UND back in the days when the Sioux played in the old Winter Sports Building. There are others like him, Grand Forks-area people who have done much on the ice and behind the scenes for Sioux hockey. 117

A good friend

Ralph Engelstad's love affair with Fighting Sioux hockey began long ago. A goalie from Thief River Falls, Minn., who played in just 14 games during his UND career from 1948 to 1950, Engelstad became a loyal fan who poured millions of dollars into the program. 120

The Grand Forks (N.D.) Herald would like to thank Kelly Sauer, assistant media relations director for UND Athletics, for her help in compiling the information for the facts & figures section.

Cliff "Fido" Purpur (to right of net with stick in hand) holds a clinic for youth in 1947 in the Winter Sports Building in Grand Forks, N.D. Purpur coached the Sioux from 1949 through 1956. Note the "fancy" chest protector worn by the goalie at left. (photo, UND Special Collections)

FRIDAY, JANUARY 9, 1948
SOUVENIR PROGRAM

HOCKEY

University of North Dakota
(Grand Forks)

VERSUS

University of Michigan
(Western Conference Champions)

Michigan Coliseum   8:00 P.M.
REFEREES................Ace Lee and Orville Roulston

MICHIGAN			NORTH DAKOTA		
No.	Name	Pos.	No.	Name	Pos.
1	Jack McDonald*	G	15	Jim Medved	C
2	Dick Starek*	LD	16	Art Forman	G
3	Connie Hill*	RD	17	Bob Murray	G
4	Leonard Brumm	RW	18	Joe Silovich	D
5	Wally Gacek*	RW	19	John Nash	W
6	Gwen McArdle	LW	20	Calvin Marvin	D
7	Gordon McMillan*	C	21	Russ Johnson	W
8	Bill Jacobson*	C	22	Gordon Christian	C
9	Al Renfrew*	LW	23	Tom Buran	
10	Ted Greer*	RW	24	Ted Dickinson	
11	Herb Upton*	RD	25	Bob Krumholtz	C
12	John Griffin	LD	26	Bill Sullivan	W
13	Sam Stedman*	C	27	Paul McKinnon	D
14	Ross Smith*	LD	28	Ed Wilson	
15	Al Nadeau	LW	29	Jim Doyle	W
16	Paul Fontana	RW	30	Wes Cole	W
18	Bob Marshall*	LD	31	Prince Johnson	W
	(* Lettermen)		32	Dan McKinnon	D

COACH..................Vic Heyliger   COACH..................Don Norman
MANAGER.............Brook Hill Snow
TRAINER...............Carl Isaacson

Next Home Game, Coliseum—UNIVERSITY of NORTH DAKOTA
Saturday, January 10, 1948—8:30 p.m.

A game program provides the details for the Jan. 9-10 series in 1948, when UND stunned the University of Michigan 6-5 on Jan. 9 in Ann Arbor. This was UND's breakthrough game into Division I, as it defeated an established college hockey power — the Wolverines.

"The people in Ann Arbor didn't know which side of the Mississippi River North Dakota was even on before we played Michigan. They know now."

Cal Marvin, principal founder of 1947-1948 team

L ong before scholarships were bountiful in college hockey, Uncle Sam's dollars helped build the foundation for Fighting Sioux hockey glory.

In the 1947-1948 season, a group of young men back from fighting for their country in World War II teamed with a few men straight out of high school to form a team that would shock the college hockey world.

"Most of us were in college on the GI bill and had jobs like sweeping the floors of the Student Union," said Cal Marvin of Warroad, Minn., a principal founder of that team. "We didn't know how good life could be."

They soon found out.

Because many of them knew each other from playing as teammates or rivals in the amateur States Dominion League in Minnesota, an idea was born.

"John Noah (Crookston, Minn.) and I were talking, and he mentioned that some guys were talking about going over to University of North Dakota and starting a college team," Marvin said.

The idea sprouted wings. Marvin and Dan McKinnon of Williams, Minn., drove to UND and flew the idea of a varsity hockey team past Glenn "Red" Jarrett, the school's athletic director.

"He said other guys had talked about it in the past but never showed up," Marvin said. "We told him we would. I give Red an awful lot of credit. He could see what was in front of him and took a gamble that we'd show up."

Jarrett promised he would build a schedule if the players showed up. He did that. UND had fielded hockey teams in the past, but none played a true collegiate schedule.

That changed when Jarrett went to work. Among the schools he scheduled were Michigan Tech, the University of Minnesota, Colorado College and the University of Michigan, all established college powers at the time.

The 1947-1948 team

Tom Buran, *Roseau, Minn.*

Gordon Christian, *Warroad, Minn.*

Wes "Frisky" Cole, *Warroad, Minn.*

Bob Dorsher, *Grand Forks, N.D.*

James Doyle, *Thief River Falls, Minn.*

Art Forman, *Wahpeton, N.D.*

Bob Grina, *Grand Forks, N.D.*

Milton "Prince" Johnson, *Webster, S.D.*

Russel "Buzz" Johnson, *Webster, S.D.*

Bobby Krumholz, *Hallock, Minn.*

Cal Marvin, *Warroad, Minn.*

Dan McKinnon, *Williams, Minn.*

Paul McKinnon, *Williams, Minn.*

Jim Medved, *Crookston, Minn.*

Bob Murray, *Warroad, Minn.*

John Noah, *Crookston, Minn.*

Joe Silovich, *Eveleth, Minn.*

Bill Sullivan, *Crookston, Minn.*

James "Itts" Williams, *Grand Forks, N.D.*

Ed Wilson, *Warroad, Minn.*

Head coach: **Don Norman**

After tuning up with four games against the Grand Forks Amerks and a Thief River Falls, Minn., team, UND's first big test came in its first game against a college opponent, the University of Michigan.

It was a daunting challenge. Michigan went on to win the 1948 NCAA championship — the first one — and won six of the first nine NCAA titles from 1948 through 1956.

The Sioux rode the train from Grand Forks to Ann Arbor, Mich., to face the powerhouse Wolverines.

Nobody gave UND a chance. How wrong they were.

Behind 34 saves from goalie Bob Murray and two goals each from Noah, Gordon "Ginny" Christian and Jim Medved, the Sioux stunned the Wolverines 6-5 to cash into big-time hockey for the first time. Noah's goal at 19:14 of the third period snapped a 5-all tie — and sent shock waves throughout college hockey.

"The people in Ann Arbor didn't know which side of the Mississippi River North Dakota was even on before we played Michigan," Marvin said. "They know now."

Dan McKinnon remembers the reception once the Sioux returned home via train.

Jarrett, in an article in the Grand Forks Herald, urged band members and "students who do not have classes Monday morning" to meet the team at the Great Northern Railway depot when they returned at 8 a.m. "It was 28 below zero when we got back to Grand Forks," McKinnon said. "What really sticks out in my mind is that Red Jarrett had the UND band out at the train depot to play for us as we got off the train. I'll never forget that. That was the first time UND had beaten a Big Ten school in any sport. It was pretty exciting."

McKinnon said the Sioux were confident. "On our way to Ann Arbor, we stopped in St. Paul, where guys like Dick Roberts and (Robert) Harris, who we knew from Warroad and Roseau, were playing for (the University of) Minnesota at the time," McKinnon said.

It wasn't fancy, but it got them there. The Sioux board a Northwest Orient Airlines flight in 1958 in Grand Forks, N.D., on their way to the NCAA tournament in Minneapolis, Minn. (photo, UND Special Collections)

Opposite: *Cal Marvin of Warroad, Minn., is credited with helping UND reach NCAA Division I hockey. (photo courtesy of Cal Marvin)*

Two of college hockey's founding fathers — Cliff "Fido" Purpur (left) and John Mariucci (right) — meet with an unidentified friend in the early 1950s. Purpur and Mariucci were once Chicago Blackhawks teammates in the National Hockey League. They made a pact to return to their home states to build hockey. Purpur returned to Grand Forks to coach at every level, and Mariucci built a powerful program at the University of Minnesota. Both are members of the U.S. Hockey Hall of Fame. (photo courtesy of Mary Purpur)

"I remember Roberts telling us that Michigan would beat us by 14 goals," McKinnon said. "But we knew Minnesota had played Michigan on even terms, and we didn't figure Roberts and Harris were any better than we were, so what the hell," McKinnon said.

While UND had none of the reputation in hockey that Michigan had, it did have some excellent players.

This was a talented collection of players, brought together by the GI bill and a desire to use that money for education and playing hockey at the same time. Three of them — Noah, Christian and Dan McKinnon — later won silver medals in hockey in the Olympic Games.

They were hockey pioneers at UND. They played in an unheated rink without artificial ice, but my how proud they were of their team — and those who have followed.

"It was some pretty humble beginnings at UND," Marvin said, "but I am so proud over what has happened the last 50-plus years."

Coach Don Norman's 1947-1948 team will be remembered for finishing with an 11-5 record, including victories over the universities of Michigan and Minnesota, Michigan Tech and Colorado College.

But it's a team that always will be remembered for upsetting Michigan to thrust UND onto the top college hockey stage.

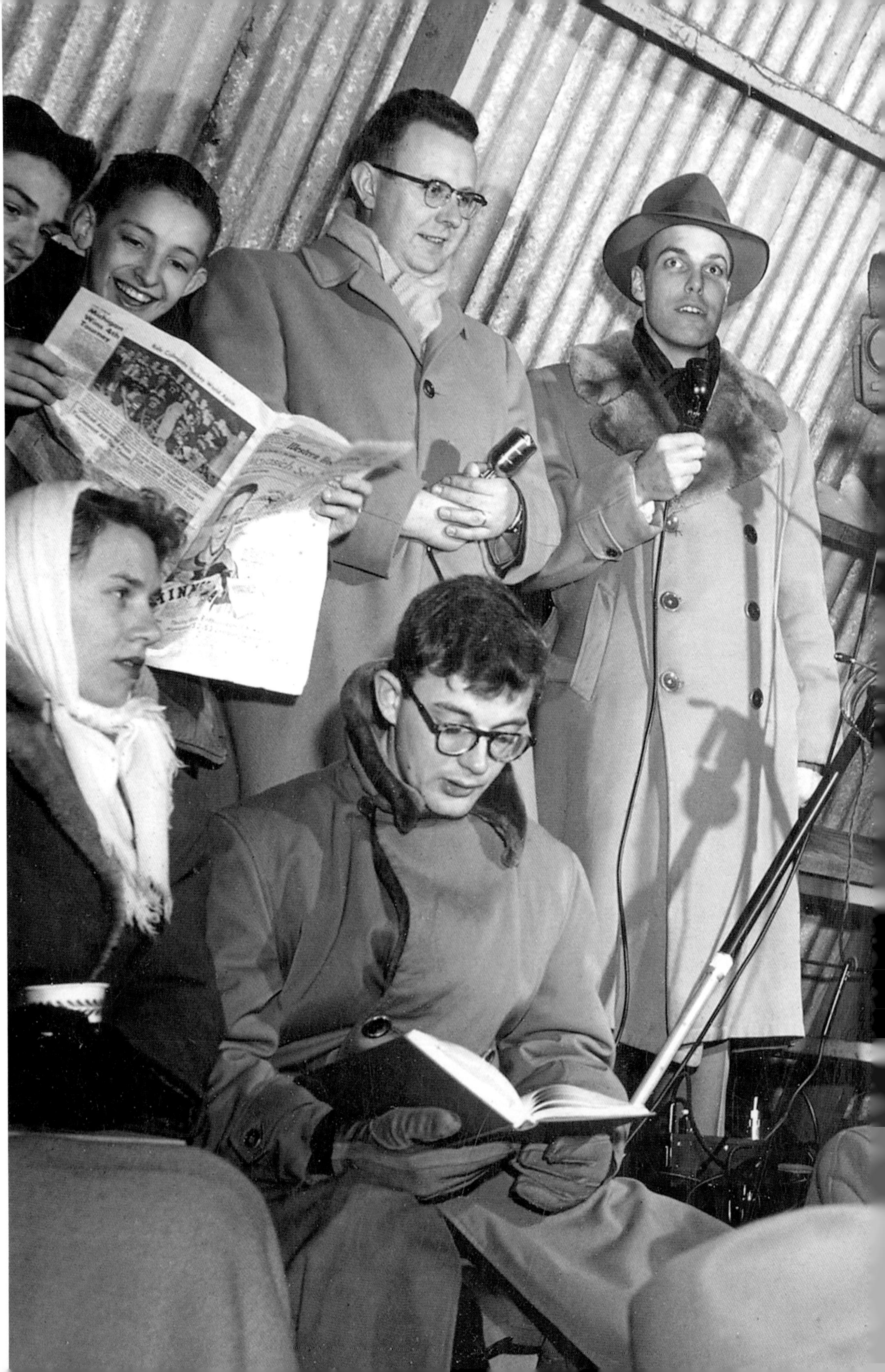

John Noah, a defenseman from Crookston, Minn., who played on the 1947-1948 Sioux team, became the first UND player to win All-America honors when he was named to the 1950-1951 team.

Taste of success *1958-1959*

UND's first NCAA championship season began with tragedy in the heat of summer in 1958 and ended in triumph in the bitter cold of winter in 1959.

Reg Morelli's overtime goal at the Houston Field House in Troy, N.Y., gave UND a 4-3 victory over Michigan State and its first NCAA championship.

But coach Bob May knew he had the makings of a championship team going into the 1958-1959 season, long before the title was claimed.

His 1957-1958 Sioux — the first of May's teams in his two years as UND's head coach — finished second in the 1958 NCAA tournament.

Yet death cast an ugly spell on the start of the 1958-1959 season, throwing things into turmoil before the first puck was dropped. That summer, arriving at UND from Canada's Northwest Territories, was a letter written in red pencil and addressed simply to "Hockey coach, UND."

It was written by the mother of Sioux sophomore goalie Tommy Forrest. "I'll never forget how it began," May said. "It said, 'My beloved Tommy was killed in a duck hunting accident,' " May recalled.

With returning goalie Bob Peabody nursing two bad knees, May needed another goalie — in a hurry. He found one on the Sioux baseball team, of all places. He talked to shortstop George Gratton from Toronto, Ont. Gratton had been cut from the hockey team the previous year when he tried out as a forward.

"George had quick hands, and he was willing to try it," May said. "That summer, we took him over to the wrestling room, which had a polished floor, and first threw tennis balls at him, then shot balls at him. We gradually got to the point where we got him on the ice — and he was pretty good."

Is togetherness a good thing? Not from the looks on the faces of these two guys. Ron King (left), a winger from Fort Frances, Ont., who played at UND from 1957 to 1960, shares time in the penalty box with an opponent in the old Winter Sports Building.
(photo courtesy of Julian Brunetta)

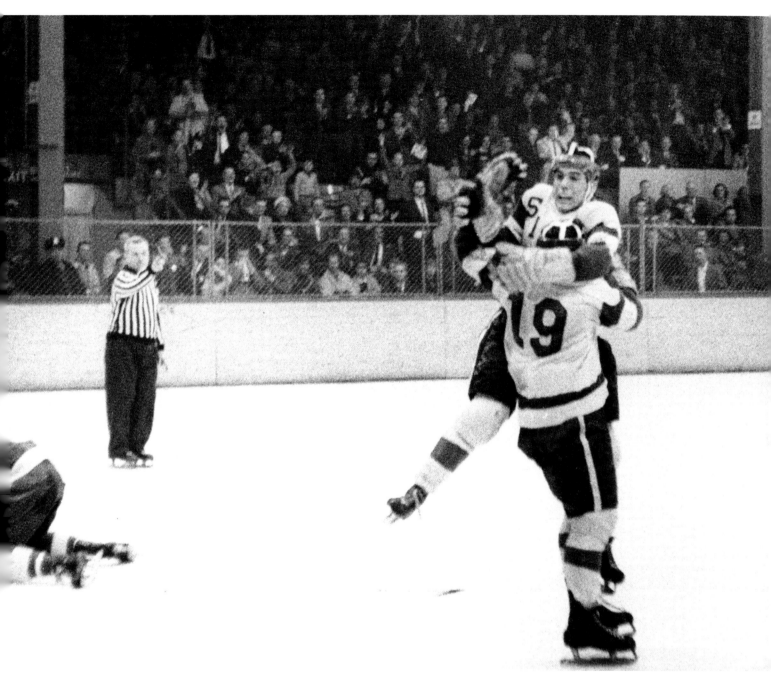

How sweet it is. Guy LaFrance makes a flying leap into the arms of teammate Reg Morelli after scoring a game-winning goal for the Fighting Sioux.
(photo courtesy of Julian Brunetta)

1958-1959 letterwinners

Bob Began, *Eveleth, Minn.*
Julian Brunetta, *Fort Frances, Ont.*
Pete Gazely, *Red Deer, Alta.*
George Gratton, *Toronto, Ont.*
Bernie Haley, *Edmonton, Alta.*
Ron King, *Fort Frances, Ont.*
Guy LaFrance, *Fort Frances, Ont.*
Bart Larson, *Minneapolis, Minn.*
Ralph Lyndon, *Winnipeg, Man.*
Les Merrifield, *Port Arthur, Ont.*
Art Miller, *Moose Jaw, Sask.*
Reg Morelli, *Hamilton, Ont.*
Stan Paschke, *Grand Forks, N.D.*
Bob Peabody, *Grand Forks, N.D.*
Garth Perry, *Red Deer, Alta.*
Joe Poole, *Thief River Falls, Minn.*
Bill Steenson, *Moose Jaw, Sask.*
Ed Thomlinson, *Sault Ste. Marie, Ont.*
Steve Thullner, *Winnipeg, Man.*
Ken Wellen, *Roseau, Minn.*
Head coach: **Bob May**
Student manager: **Ted Kotyk**

Though Peabody started the championship game victory over Michigan State, Gratton was in goal when Morelli's rebound goal gave the Sioux their first title. He had come on in the third period after Peabody had given up two goals, allowing the Spartans to rally from a 3-1 deficit.

The championship literally was built from the ground up.

The summer before the season started, Sioux players Art Miller and Don Crow rebuilt the locker room, using donated lumber, making individual stalls for each player.

Maybe being the first national champion at UND built the bond the team has to this day. Most remain in touch and get together once a year at coach May's home in the Twin Cities.

But May did a lot to cement that bond when he coached them, too. "We put on an alumni game to help raise money for our team, and such former Sioux stars as Ben Cherski and Ken Johannson came back to play in it," May said. "The proceeds we raised from that, we used to buy green blazers and gray slacks for each player. Maybe that helped build the Fighting Sioux spirit."

That spirit was needed. Bill Steenson, an All-America defenseman selection the previous two seasons, was declared academically ineligible at the end of the first semester, along with Steve Thullner, another defenseman.

Even so, the Sioux pressed on through other unusual circumstances. A Jan. 16 game between UND and the University of Michigan in Grand Forks was called off with 5:20 remaining in the game because of a fight involving players and fans. Officially, the game went down as a 6-1 Sioux victory.

Nearly 6,000 fans watched the title game in Troy, though no East Coast team was in the finals. But the tournament had none of the electric

During the championship 1958-1959 season, the Sioux won 20 games and lost just 10, so celebrations took place more often than not. Here, Steve Thullner (3), Reg Morelli (16) and goalie Bob Peabody gather for congratulations after a UND victory. (photo courtesy of Bob Peabody)

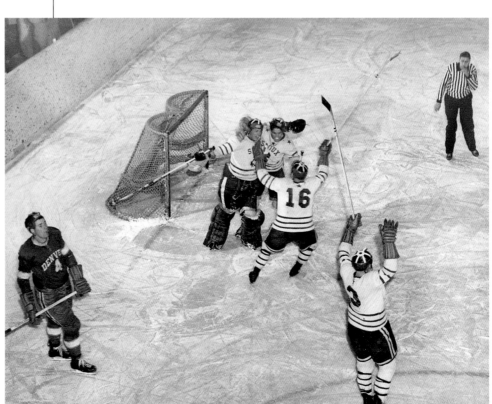

Bill Steenson was a two-time All-America selection on defense for UND.

Ed Thomlinson (left), a wing from Sault Ste. Marie, Ont., celebrates his goal against the Minnesota Gophers during the 1958-1959 season. Thomlinson scored 49 goals in 95 games during his three seasons with the Sioux varsity. (photo, UND Special Collections)

Bob May wasn't head coach at UND for long, guiding the Sioux from 1957 through 1959. But he left his mark as a coach, winning the NCAA title in 1959 in Troy, N.Y. May's Sioux won both games in overtime in the 1959 Frozen Four, as UND picked up its first national championship in hockey. (photo, UND Athletics)

atmosphere of today's NCAA tournaments, which are played in front of nearly three times as many fans.

At the 2001 NCAA tournament held in Albany, N.Y., just a few miles from Troy, nearly 300 press members were on hand.

In 1959? "I remember there was one guy (Jim Hansen) from the Grand Forks newspaper," Sioux player Ed Thomlinson recalled. "I don't remember seeing too many others."

May does remember how they helped Ron King, a young forward from Fort Frances, Ont., overcome his nervousness.

"He'd be so nervous before a game that he couldn't even lace on his skates," May said. "So our team doctor (Jim Leigh) would give him a pill and a cup of water before every game and tell him they were 'Bud Wilkinson butterfly tablets.' " Wilkinson was the football coach at Oklahoma University at the time.

Those tablets calmed King's butterflies. King took the pills, laced on his skates and played a big role in the title run, assisting on one of UND's goals in the title game. And the pills? "They were nothing but salt tablets," May said.

May left UND after the 1958-1959 season to coach the Denver Mavericks of the International League. He didn't want to leave UND, but with a young daughter born with cerebral palsy, the medical facilities in Denver were better suited to address her needs.

May himself wanted to become a physician. But once he made that decision at age 31, he said that Grand Forks doctor Edgar Haunz convinced him he was too old to pursue that profession.

So, May became a dentist. He continues to follow UND hockey closely. He admits he misses the days of coaching the Fighting Sioux. "I wish I had stayed at UND," May says now. "That is true."

25

1959

Houston Field House

Troy, N.Y.

March 14, 1959

North Dakota 4, Michigan State 3 (OT)

UND strikes gold. Coach Bob May's Sioux top Michigan State 4-3 in overtime in Troy, N.Y., on March 14, 1959, for UND's first national title. Reg Morelli, the tournament's Most Outstanding Player, scores the overtime winner.
(photo, UND Athletics)

Reg Morelli became an instant hero in UND history and the Most Outstanding Player in the NCAA tournament all in one swing of his stick.

Morelli's goal at four minutes and 18 seconds of overtime, on a play set up by linemate Art Miller, gave the Sioux a 4-3 victory over Michigan State and brought UND its first NCAA championship.

Morelli put in a rebound to win it after the Spartans had struck for two third-period goals to rally from a 3-1 deficit and force overtime. Ralph Lyndon, Gerry Walford and Stan Paschke scored goals in a span of 136 seconds midway through the second period to wipe out Michigan State's 1-0 lead after one period.

In addition to the tournament

Most Outstanding Player award given to Morelli, his name has remained in the forefront in Sioux hockey lore.

"If I knew he'd get all that attention," Miller said, joking. "I'd have scored the goal myself."

The Sioux had beaten St. Lawrence from nearby Canton, N.Y., by an identical 4-3 overtime margin in the semifinals. Guy LaFrance's goal at 4:22 of OT, knocked out the team with the largest fan support.

Morelli scored two goals, and Miller and LaFrance one each in the win over St. Lawrence.

Even with St. Lawrence eliminated, nearly 6,000 fans — described by Grand Forks (N.D.)

Herald sportswriter Jim Hansen as "pro-North Dakota" — jammed the Houston Field House for the championship game.

Coach Bob May described his team at the time as "the best I have ever coached from the standpoint of spirit and desire to win."

Hansen's story on the title game in the Herald began this way: "The hockey spotlight beamed brightly on the University of North Dakota today following the sensational Sioux 4-3 overtime triumph over Michigan State Saturday night, which brought the school its first national collegiate hockey championship."

The Sioux and the Spartans had met four times previously that season, each winning twice. But the biggest game of all — for the NCAA title — swung in UND's favor.

Morelli was joined on the all-tournament team by linemate Ed Thomlinson, with Sioux forward Joe Poole and defenseman Lyndon named to the second team.

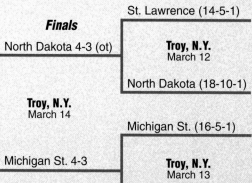

Finals

North Dakota 4-3 (ot)

North Dakota 4-3 (ot)
National champion

Michigan St. 4-3

Semifinals

St. Lawrence (14-5-1)

Troy, N.Y.
March 12

North Dakota (18-10-1)

Troy, N.Y.
March 14

Michigan St. (16-5-1)

Troy, N.Y.
March 13

Boston College (19-7)

Inside the game

Saves: North Dakota (George Gratton, 21); Michigan State (Joe Selinger, 26).
Total penalties: North Dakota 9 for 18 minutes; Michigan State 8 for 16 minutes.
Power plays: North Dakota 0 for 5; Michigan State 0 for 5.
Officials: Bob Barry, Vince Riley.

1st

Goals
1. MS, Ed Pollesell (Tom Mustonen, Andre LaCoste) 14:38.
Penalties
MS, Robert Armstrong (cross checking) 8:42; MS, E. Pollesell (slashing) 15:40; ND, Ralph Lyndon (interference) 18:32.

2nd

Goals
2. ND, Lyndon (Reg Morelli, Art Miller) 7:21; 3. ND, Gerry Walford (Ron King, Bernie Haley) 8:57; 4. ND, Stan Paschke (Lyndon), 9:37.
Penalties
ND, Miller (tripping) 4:11; ND, Morelli (hooking) 11:19; MS, Bob Norman (cross checking) 12:43; ND, Miller (roughing) 13:28; MS, Bruno Pollesell (roughing) 13:28; ND, Guy LaFrance (tripping) 15:29; ND, Julian Brunetta (interference) 16:47.

3rd

Goals
5. MS, LaCoste (Jack Roberts, Norman) 8:05; 6. MS, Roberts (LaCoste) 16:20.
Penalties
ND, Brunetta (high sticking) 4:36; MS, Norman (high sticking) 4:36; MS, E. Pollesell (tripping) 8:49; MS, Norman (high sticking) 16:38; ND, Les Merrifield (interference) 16:38.

OT

Goals
7. ND, Morelli (Miller, LaFrance) 4:18.
Penalties
MS, Tom Mustonen (tripping) 3:01; ND, Lyndon (tripping) 3:13.

At Grand Forks (N.D.) International Airport in 1963,
hundreds of fans gather to eagerly await the arrival
of the Fighting Sioux hockey team from Chestnut Hill,
Mass. The Sioux beat Denver University 6-5 in the
title game to give the school its second national
championship. (photo, UND Special Collections)

Al McLean, who scored UND's key sixth goal in the 1963 championship game, was a first-team All-American. He scored two goals in the final — a 6-5 victory over Denver (Colo.) University.

Revenge: Title No. 2 *1962-1963*

It was difficult to tell which was worse.

Was it the pain in the lungs and legs of the UND players after losing a tough overtime game against a strong Denver (Colo.) University team in Denver's high altitude?

Or was it the pain UND's players felt after the game ended? How hurtful was it for them to stand on the ice when the game was over, and they had lost? How painful was it for them to watch Denver being presented with the MacNaughton Cup as Western Collegiate Hockey Association playoff champions?

The pain was felt in every aspect. But it was the agony of the 5-4 overtime loss to the Pioneers on March 9, 1963, that turned into ecstasy a week later in Chestnut Hill, Mass.

"I'll never forget that loss in Denver," said Don Ross, an All-American defenseman for the Sioux that season. "We were all pretty disappointed. That game brought us a lot of quiet resolve. Standing on the ice when it was over and watching them (the Pioneers) receiving the trophy, that was our incentive if we met them again."

They did meet again, this time for far greater stakes. In the NCAA championship game in Chestnut Hill, the Sioux blasted coach Murray Armstrong's Denver team for three goals in the first eight minutes in skating to a 6-5 win, capturing UND's second NCAA championship.

Barry Thorndycraft was in the fourth year of his five-year run as Sioux head coach.

As coach of the freshman team earlier, he had brought in players such as Ross, Al McLean and Dave Merrifield, all stars on the 1963 championship team.

By NCAA rules, freshmen were ineligible for varsity competition. But when his freshmen scrimmaged against the Sioux varsity, Thorndycraft knew he had something special.

1962-1963 letterwinners

George Baland, *Virginia, Minn.*
Bob Bartlett, *Edmonton, Alta.*
Bill Borlase, *Fort Frances, Ont.*
George Chigol, *Flin Flon, Man.*
Ernie Dyda, *Norquay, Sask.*
George Goodacre, *Red Deer, Alta.*
Wayne Gurba, *Flin Flon, Man.*
Joe Lech, *Glen Bain, Sask.*
Jack Matheson, *Brandon, Man.*
Al McLean, *New Westminster, B.C.*
Dave Merrifield, *Port Arthur, Ont.*
Dudley Gene Otto, *South St. Paul, Minn.*
Maurice Roberge, *Edmonton, Alta.*
Don Ross, *Roseau, Minn.*
Bill Selman, *Fort Frances, Ont.*
Pete Stasiuk, *Lethbridge, Alta.*
Arnold Steeves, *Tacoma, Wash.*
Wilmot Stirrett, *Port Arthur, Ont.*
Don Stokaluk, *Port Arthur, Ont.*
Dan Storsteen, *Devils Lake, N.D.*
John Sutherland, *Winnipeg, Man.*
Head coach: **Barry Thorndycraft**
Assistant coach: **Bob Peters**
Student manager: **Murray Olson**

A UND student pauses outside a campus display to read a Dakota Student newspaper account of UND's victory in the 1963 NCAA championship game. (photo, UND Special Collections)

"Our freshman team could beat our varsity team," Thorndycraft said. So, expectations were high when Thorndycraft replaced Bob May as coach to start the 1959-1960 season. Nobody expected more than Thorndycraft, a Winnipeg, Man., native who was an assistant coach under May on UND's 1959 NCAA championship team.

When both his 1960-1961 and 1961-1962 teams struggled to sub-.500 seasons, Thorndycraft wasn't happy. He let his players know that, time and again.

"I'll never forget one time in the locker room when coach got on us, because we hadn't lived up to what we thought we could do, since our freshman year," Ross said.

"In a way, we felt he jumped off the bandwagon. I remember that Al McLean stood up and said, 'Why don't you give us a chance?,' and Barry shut up. He never said another negative thing the rest of the year."

On March 16, 1963, in Chestnut Hill, it came time for the Sioux to put up or shut up for good.

Using a swarming, aggressive forechecking system favored by Thorndycraft, the Sioux smothered Denver, outshooting the Pioneers 39-17.

"Leaky Joe" Lech, UND's goalie, stopped just 12 shots, allowing five pucks to go by him.

"I'd never seen him play before we recruited him," Thorndycraft said. "He played on a bad team before he came to UND. He'd face 50 shots in a game and give up five goals. The problem was, when he faced 17 shots, he'd still give up five. When we had the 6-5 lead on Denver, I think our players would have killed him if he had given up another goal."

UND whipped Boston College 8-2 in the NCAA semifinals, earning rave reviews from Boston College coach John "Snooks" Kelly.

"North Dakota has a great team," Kelly said afterward. "They could blow you clean out of the country with their explosive attack."

At the time, it was rare for a college player to go on to the NHL, which had just six teams. "Nowadays," Thorndycraft said, "if you can skate from one end of the rink to the other without falling down, you can play in the NHL. By today's standards, Don Ross would have gone right to the NHL and been a star. He, along with McLean and Merrifield, were my best players."

George Starcher, UND's president at the time, had faith in the Sioux. The afternoon before the title game, Starcher sent a telegram to the Sioux team and UND athletic director Len Marti, telling them to keep the game-winning puck, which would be placed in a cornerstone at Twamley Hall on UND's campus.

"Everyone back in North Dakota should be proud of these kids as great hockey players and also as great gentlemen off the ice," Marti said

They're back! Head coach Barry Thorndycraft (glasses, top) and captain Maurice Roberge (carrying trophy) step off the plane in Grand Forks, N.D., after the Sioux return from winning the 1963 NCAA tournament in Chestnut Hill, Mass. (photo, UND Special Collections)

after the title game — with the game-winning puck safely tucked into his pocket.

Thorndycraft, a Canadian, had a temporary visa that allowed him to coach at UND, but he eventually ran afoul with immigration laws. UND appealed his case all the way to Washington, D.C., in an effort to get a permanent visa for him, but without success.

So, one year after coaching UND to the NCAA championship in 1963, Thorndycraft left the school, going to Switzerland to coach a professional hockey team.

"I could have renewed my temporary visa at UND if I had wanted to," Thorndycraft said. "But I figured I had done all I could at UND — so I left."

But before he did, he left UND the legacy of its second NCAA championship.

1963

McHugh Forum
Chestnut Hill, Mass.
March 16, 1963

North Dakota 6, Denver 5

Coach Barry Thorndycraft, an assistant coach on the 1959 national championship team, wins his only NCAA title as head coach at UND on March 16, 1963. The Sioux shade Denver (Colo.) University 6-5 in Chestnut Hill, Mass., with Al McLean being named the tournament's Most Outstanding Player.
(photo, UND Athletics)

The Grand Forks (N.D.) Herald account of the game by sportswriter Jim Hansen on March 17 told it all.

"Revenge was sweet for UND Saturday night as the Sioux turned back Denver (Colo.) University 6-5 to win the NCAA hockey championship before 'home' fans at McHugh Forum," Hansen wrote.

The Sioux, picked by league coaches to finish fourth in the Western Collegiate Hockey Association, tied for first place during the regular season with Denver.

But in the league playoffs, Denver stopped UND 5-4 in overtime in Denver to capture the play-off title.

One week after the tough overtime loss in the WCHA play-

off finals, the Sioux sought revenge. They got it in the form of a flurry of goals that stunned the Pioneers, leaving them reeling before the game was eight minutes old.

Goals by Don Stokaluk at 1:57 of the opening period were followed by goals from Al McLean at 3:11 and Ernie Dyda at 7:25, much to the delight of 4,200 fans, most of them cheering for the Sioux.

The 3-0 North Dakota lead was too much for Denver. The Pioneers closed the gap to 3-2 late in the first period. But Stokaluk scored his second goal of the game at 14:20, and Jack Matheson made it 5-2 less than a minute later.

McLean's second goal made

it 6-2 at 5:01 of the second period. Bob Hamill's goal at 13:09 of the second period cut the lead to 6-3, and goals by Greg Lacomy and Hamill in the third period closed the margin even more.

UND outshot Denver 39-17, as Sioux goalie Joe Lech made just 12 saves.

"Playing cautiously in the final 20 minutes, North Dakota allowed just two shots on goal in the last period," Hansen wrote, "but the first by Hamill went in from about 40 feet, giving the junior wing a hat trick."

McLean was named tournament Most Outstanding Player. Joining him on the all-tournament first team were Don Ross, Stokaluk, George Goodacre and Dave Merrifield.

McLean joined defenseman Ross and Merrifield in earning All-America honors.

To Merrifield, all the Sioux were stars. "We've got 20 All-Americans on this club," he said. "This has to be the biggest thrill of my life."

Semifinals

North Dakota (20-7-3)

Chestnut Hill, Mass.
March 14

Boston College (22-7)

Finals

North Dakota 8-2

Denver (22-8-1)

Chestnut Hill, Mass.
March 15

Clarkson (19-3-2)

North Dakota 6-5

National champion

Chestnut Hill, Mass.
March 16

Denver 6-2

Inside the game

Saves: North Dakota (Joe Lech,12); Denver (Rudy Unis, 33).
Total penalties: North Dakota 5 for 10 minutes; Denver 3 for 6 minutes.
Power plays: North Dakota 1 for 3; Denver 2 for 5.
Attendance: 4,200.

1st

Goals
1. ND, Don Stokaluk (Dave Merrifield, Bob Bartlett) 1:57; 2. ND, Al McLean (Bartlett, John Sutherland) 3:11; 3. ND, Ernie Dyda (Jack Matheson, Merrifield) 7:25 (sh); 4. D, Greg Lacomy (Jim Kenning, Dom Fragomeni) 12:55; 5. D, Bob Hamill (Jack Wilson, Jon Art) 13:13; 6. ND, Stokaluk (Maurice Roberge) 14:20; 7. ND, Matheson (Don Ross) 15:14.
Penalties
ND, George Goodacre (cross checking) 6:17.

2nd

Goals
8. ND, McLean (unassisted) 5:01 (pp); 9. D, Lacomy (Wilson, Marshall Johnston) 7:05 (pp); 10. D, Hamill (Billy Staub) 13:09 (pp).
Penalties
D, Lacomy (holding) 3:15; ND, Roberge (holding) 5:17; ND, Matheson (tripping) 10:10; ND, Matheson (tripping) 12:25.

3rd

Goals
11. D, Hamill (Doug Kowel, Lawrence John) 13:19.
Penalties
D, Johnston (tripping) 3:11; ND, Bartlett (holding) 4:51; D, Kowel (interference) 6:19.

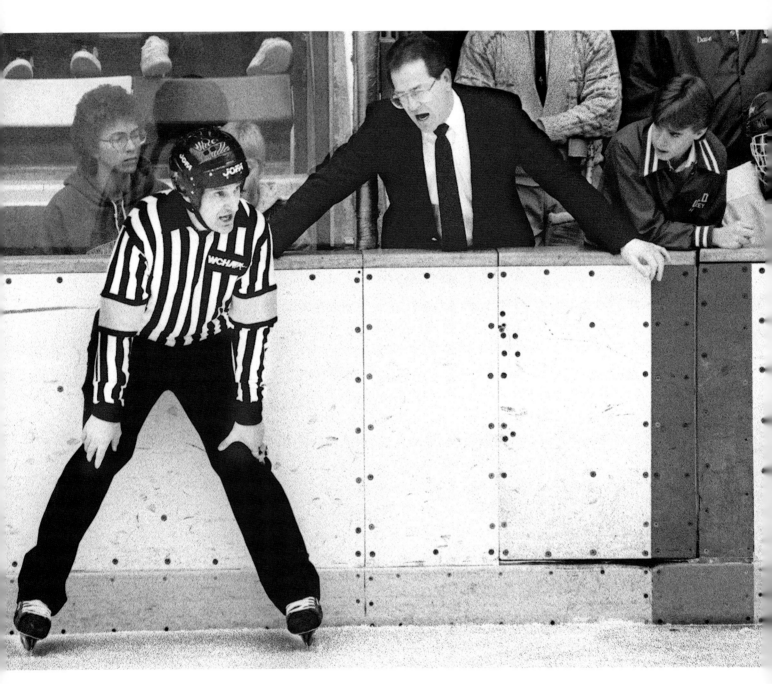

And furthermore! UND coach John "Gino" Gasparini gives referee Medo Martinello his interpretation of how the game should be officiated during this 1989 contest at UND. Judging by the expressions of Gasparini and the referee, the discussion isn't going well. (photo, Jackie Lorentz, Grand Forks Herald)

All Gino did was win *1978-1994*

UND's hiring of John "Gino" Gasparini on March 7, 1978, and his firing on April 9, 1994, both were clouded in controversy.

But in his 16 years as head coach of the Fighting Sioux, the Fort Frances, Ont., native left a legacy that has been matched only rarely in college hockey.

He not only finished his career as UND's winningest hockey coach (392-248-24, .608), but he won more NCAA titles (three) than any other Sioux coach. In the entire history of college hockey, only the University of Michigan's Vic Heyliger (six titles) and Denver's Murray Armstrong (five) have won more NCAA crowns than Gasparini-coached teams.

His career as a player, assistant coach and then as head coach at UND spanned 30 years. Those years included some of the more remarkable teams and memorable moments in Sioux history.

As great as his legacy is, one fact easily is overlooked.

Nearly 30 young men who either played for him or were assistant coaches under him moved on in the game as scouts, high school, college or pro coaches, or coached in the United States Hockey League, the prime developmental league for college players.

"That's a true testament to the coaching side of Gino," former Sioux player Cary Eades said.

Eades should know. He saw all sides of Gasparini, first as a player on Gasparini's first team, as co-captain of his second NCAA title team in 1982 and as an assistant coach under Gasparini.

"Gino has the ability to develop leaders and give the leaders a lot of ownership in the team," said Eades, who has seen the game as a coach in high school (Warroad, Minn.) and as a head coach in the USHL.

"There's no question that he was a dictator, that he was the boss," Eades said. "At the same time, he gave his leaders that ownership in the team, so a unique relationship developed. Maybe that sprung forth in the desire of so many of us to coach."

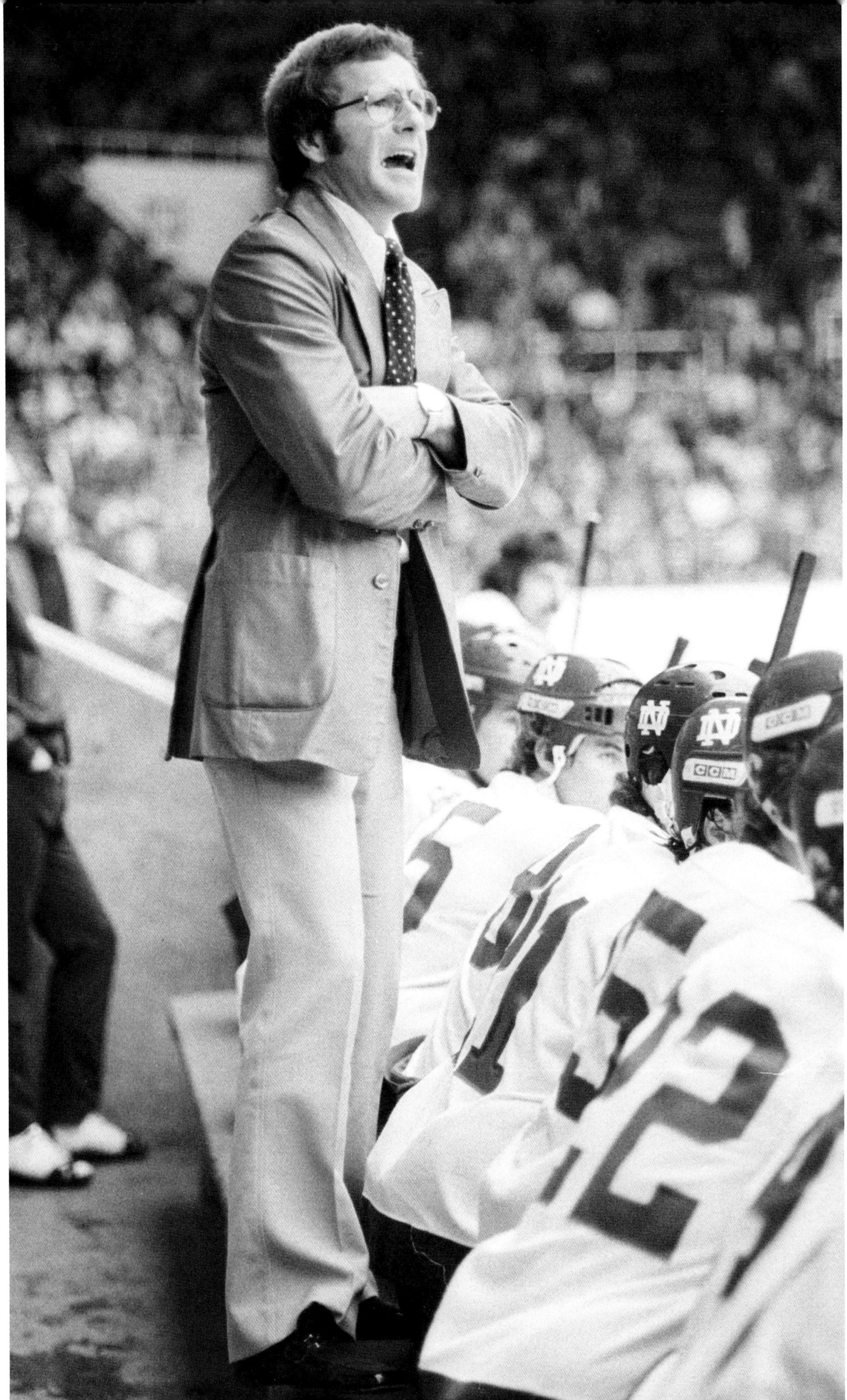
CCM

Gasparini may have been a dictator as a coach, but his recruiting prowess was legendary.

Take his class that came during the fall of 1981. All six freshmen who played on the 1981-1982 NCAA championship team eventually went on to play in the National Hockey League.

The six were Jim Archibald, Dave Donnelly, James Patrick, Gord Sherven, Dave Tippett and Rick Zombo. Patrick still is active in the NHL with the Buffalo Sabres, and Tippett is involved as assistant coach with the NHL's Los Angeles Kings.

Gasparini felt that discipline was paramount. He ruled with the iron hand that Eades said he did. "Inmates don't run the asylum," Gasparini said.

When Gasparini applied to be head coach in 1978, he was not the leading candidate. In fact, of the three finalists, he generally was regarded as No. 3.

But top choice Marshall Johnston of Denver, Colo., pulled out because his wife didn't want to move to Grand Forks, N.D. And the next

Gino Gasparini served as a tri-captain of the Sioux in 1967-1968, his senior season. He was a longtime assistant coach under Rube Bjorkman and head coach at UND from 1978 through 1994. There hasn't been much that's happened in Fighting Sioux hockey that Gasparini hasn't seen. (photo, John Stennes, Grand Forks Herald)

choice, Ned Harkness, asked too much from UND. Though Harkness won NCAA titles at both Rensselaer (N.Y.) Polytechnic Institute and Cornell University in Ithaca, N.Y., UND athletic director Carl Miller eventually balked at Harkness' demands.

So Gasparini, the ex-Sioux player and longtime assistant under Rube Bjorkman, got the job more by default than as a first choice.

Whatever the reason, the end results turned out to be golden for UND. Gasparini resurrected the status of Sioux hockey and took it to the top, to the point that UND's hockey program was named No. 1 in the United States by The Hockey News in the early 1980s.

Gasparini drove himself hard, his players even harder.

"A lot of players despised him, because he'd get in their faces big-time," Eades said. "He'd push them to levels they never thought possible. Some players respectfully hated him, some respectfully loved him — but every player respected him for being a tough taskmaster."

That was by design. "If you don't have leadership," Gasparini said, "it's like the old saying about straightening out the deck chairs on the Titanic."

Gasparini's ship floated high and mighty during much of his reign before running into choppy waters near the end.

"One thing about Gino is that he came to the job with great vision," Eades said. "He had this vision of restoring Sioux hockey to what it enjoyed in the late 1950s and early 1960s. He talked about bringing respect back to the program a lot."

The respect came instantly. In Gasparini's first year as head coach, the Sioux won the Western Collegiate Hockey Association title. The Sioux rolled all the way to the NCAA championship game before losing to the University of Minnesota Gophers.

"It was so fun watching it all develop," Gasparini said. "We had seniors (in 1978-1979) like Bill Himmelright, who had never experienced winning to this extent, so it was fun for all."

The Sioux learned to win under Gasparini, and he learned as well. His assistants in the 1978-1979 season were Rick Wilson and Bill Wilkinson. "We were learning all together," Gasparini said. "We were making a name for ourselves as a team and learning as we went along. I remember our famous statement among the three of us:

"We'd look at each other and say, 'What next?' " Gasparini said.

What was next were national championships in 1980, 1982 and 1987 and national coach of the year honors for Gasparini in 1987, when the Sioux won an NCAA-record 40 games.

Gasparini recruited so well that he drew major attention in Canada. The Edmonton (Alta.) Journal newspaper once ran a lengthy feature on Gasparini, along with a photograph of the coach wearing his trademark trench coat while scouting for talent at an Alberta rink.

"Why is this little man in a trench coat stealing all of Alberta's best players?" the headline asked.

Gino Gasparini and UND President Tom Clifford share a personal conversation. Under Clifford's tenure as president, Gasparini served for a while in a dual role as hockey coach and athletic director. (photo, John Stennes, Grand Forks Herald)

Gino Gasparini was named coach of the year in the WCHA three times — in 1979, 1982 and 1987 — and won the Spencer Penrose Award as national coach of the year in 1987.

Why indeed. Because he could and because he went hard after top players. It didn't matter to Gasparini how long they stayed at UND. He recruited top talent — high-profile players such as Troy Murray, Doug Smail, Dave Tippett, Dave Donnelly, Perry Berezan, Kevin Maxwell, James Patrick, Gord Sherven, Howard Walker, Tony Hrkac, Bob Joyce, Ian Kidd and Ed Belfour — molded them into national championship teams, and then wished them well when they left UND early to go to the NHL.

"Gino never stood in a player's way," Eades said. "He was interested in what they could add to the program at UND, but he had the life interest of the young players at heart, too. When it came time for them to move on, he'd shake their hand and thank them for what they did for UND."

Gasparini sent 40 players to the NHL. He was raided early and often, 22 of his players leaving early to sign professional contracts. It makes one wonder just how many more titles Gasparini might have won if all his talent had stayed around for four seasons.

Gasparini had a chance to move on, too. He was once a serious candidate to go to the NHL as a coach.

Then, after three losing seasons from 1991 through 1994, Gasparini was dismissed as coach by UND athletic director Terry Wanless.

Gasparini's ex-players were incensed, filling the mailbag of the Grand Forks Herald and flooding the newspaper with phone calls.

But he was thankful for having the opportunity to coach his alma mater.

"I look back, and I am most grateful for a guy like (UND President) Tom Clifford, who was a key element in that whole scenario of

Gino Gasparini runs the Sioux through their paces, barking out instructions. (photo, John Stennes, Grand Forks Herald)

Opposite: *Laughing all the way to the bank? Not quite, certainly not yet. But coach Gasparini (right) and team captain Cary Eades share a happy moment as the Sioux tune up for the 1982 NCAA championship game in Providence, R.I. The happiness carries through, as the Sioux beat Wisconsin 5-2 for the victory. (photo, bill alkofer, Dakota Student)*

my hiring in 1978," Gasparini said. "Whether it was a process of elimination or attrition when I got the job, it makes no difference to me.

"Now, that's just a blurp in my career and memories. There are a lot of second, third choices in every phase of life. The key is what you do with your opportunity."

When Gasparini was let go, there was a tremendous amount of anger directed at Wanless and UND by former players and fans.

"I look back at that, and I think it's part of the loyalty the players have," Gasparini said. "I spent 30 some years where everything in the hockey program at UND was a priority in our lives.

"All of a sudden, it stopped dead. I got off. The train went the other way, and so did I."

Gasparini became commissioner of the United States Hockey League, and that's been rewarding, too. The USHL is a top feeder program for the Western Collegiate Hockey Association and other Division I leagues.

So, instead of coaching college players, he's helping to groom prospects for the leap to major college hockey. Under Gasparini, the league has continued to flourish.

"I've had as much satisfaction in this job as I did coaching at UND," he said.

In his 16 years as head coach, he had winning records in 13, winning four WCHA titles to go with three NCAA crowns.

From 1984 to 1990, he served as both head hockey coach and athletic director at UND. He resigned as athletic director in 1990.

"I went through a whole lot of staff changes in hockey, so I felt I had to make a choice," Gasparini said.

He rebuilt his coaching staff, but he couldn't rebuild the program fast enough to suit Wanless. "When you're down, you don't get back up as quickly as you'd like," Gasparini said.

Gasparini's run as UND's head coach ended with his dismissal in 1994.

"It's history, and it's gone," Gasparini said. "Let's just say that if I was in that position making that decision, I would have never done it that way."

Gasparini said other coaches called to thank him.

"They said that after what happened to me at UND, they got 20 percent raises and increases in the length of their contracts," Gasparini said. "I told them that was great."

Still, Gasparini's legacy lives on today.

UND head coach Dean Blais was once an assistant under Gasparini. And Blais' two assistants, Brad Berry and Dave Hakstol, were former players at UND under Gasparini.

So, while Gasparini has moved on, his restoration project of rebuilding Sioux hockey goes on and on.

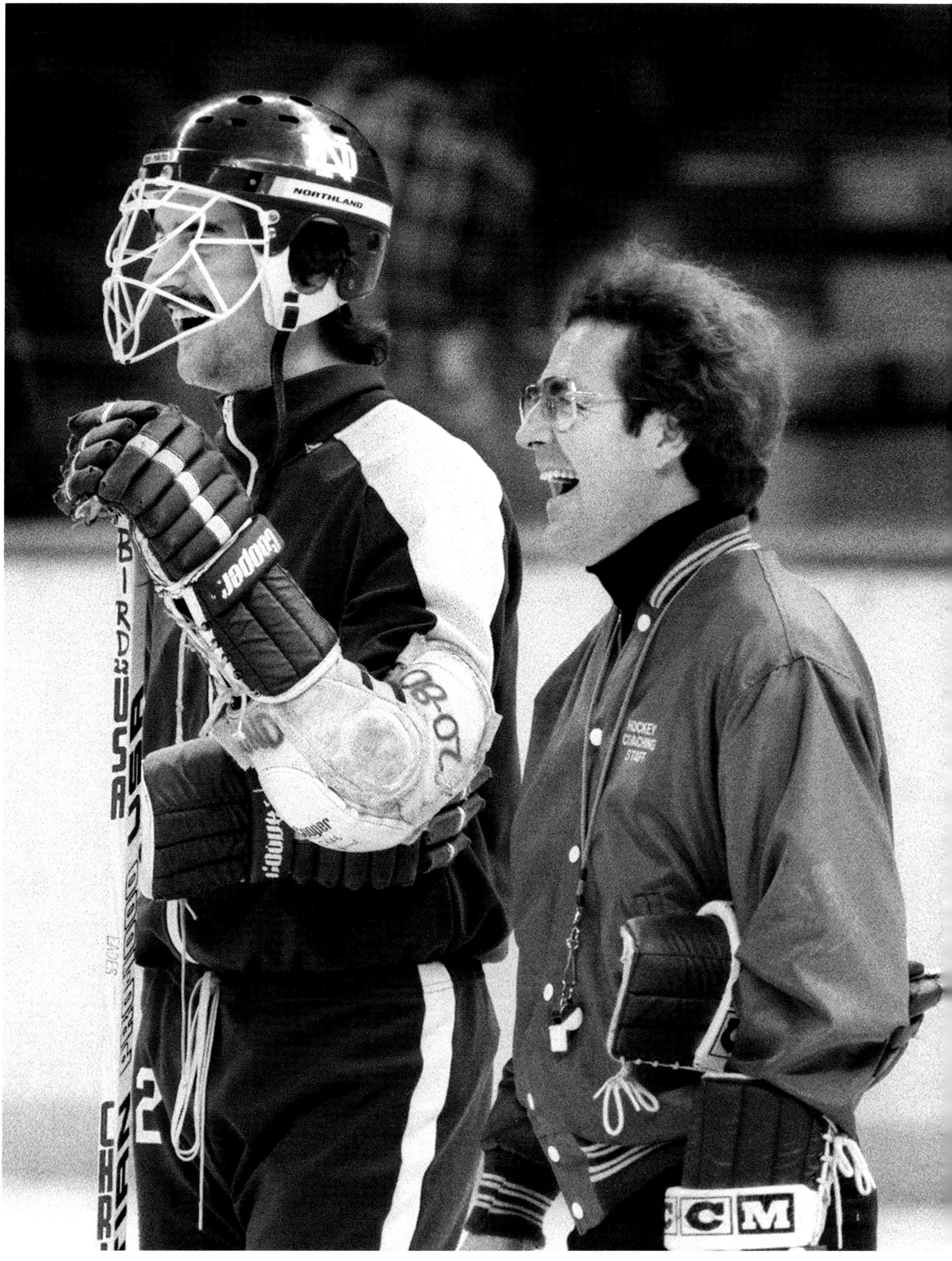
NORTHLAND
USA
HOCKEY
COACHING
STAFF
CCM

Inevitable champions *1979-1980*

There were handshakes and hugs all around when the Sioux won the 1980 NCAA championship in Providence, R.I. Here, Frank Burggraf (left) celebrates the triumph with senior defenseman Travis Dunn. (photo, John Stennes, Grand Forks Herald)

Opposite: *Some 20 years ago, Kermit the Frog took on an unofficial role as mascot of the Sioux. It was appropriate enough, because it was during the late 1970s and early 1980s that Sioux hockey took a giant leap forward. (photo, John Stennes, Grand Forks Herald)*

The 1980 Fighting Sioux took second-year head coach John "Gino" Gasparini to the top of the hockey world in a hurry, winning the school's first NCAA title since 1963.

Yet, in a sense, it was a team that later left him wondering why they hadn't won more than 31 games.

"That was a very skilled team," Gasparini said. "It was good enough that it could have gone undefeated."

It was a team (31-8-1) that closed with a rush. The Sioux won their last 14 games, blowing away Michigan State and Notre Dame in the Western Collegiate Hockey Association playoffs to advance to the NCAA tournament in Providence, R.I.

Once there, the pummeling continued. The Sioux beat New Hampshire's Dartmouth College 4-1 in the semifinals, then blitzed Northern Michigan 5-2 in the championship game. In a remarkable performance, tournament Most Outstanding Player Doug Smail, the little guy from Moose Jaw, Sask., with a booming shot and jets for skates, scored four of UND's five goals.

The victory over Northern Michigan was sweet revenge for the Sioux. On the first weekend in January that season, the Sioux went to Marquette, Mich., ranked No. 1 nationally, but they were swept by coach Rick Comley's Wildcats.

When the Sioux arrived at their hotel for that weekend, the hotel billboard had a welcoming sign congratulating the Sioux for being "No. 1 in the nation." But after the Sioux lost twice to Northern Michigan and before they even got back to their hotel after the second game, the billboard sign had been changed.

It now read, "Congratulations, Wildcats!"

Three months later in Providence, the Sioux turned the tables.

This was a Sioux team that could play any style successfully. UND could be smooth and cool, rough and physical or a combination of all.

"They dictated how they wanted the game to be played," Gasparini

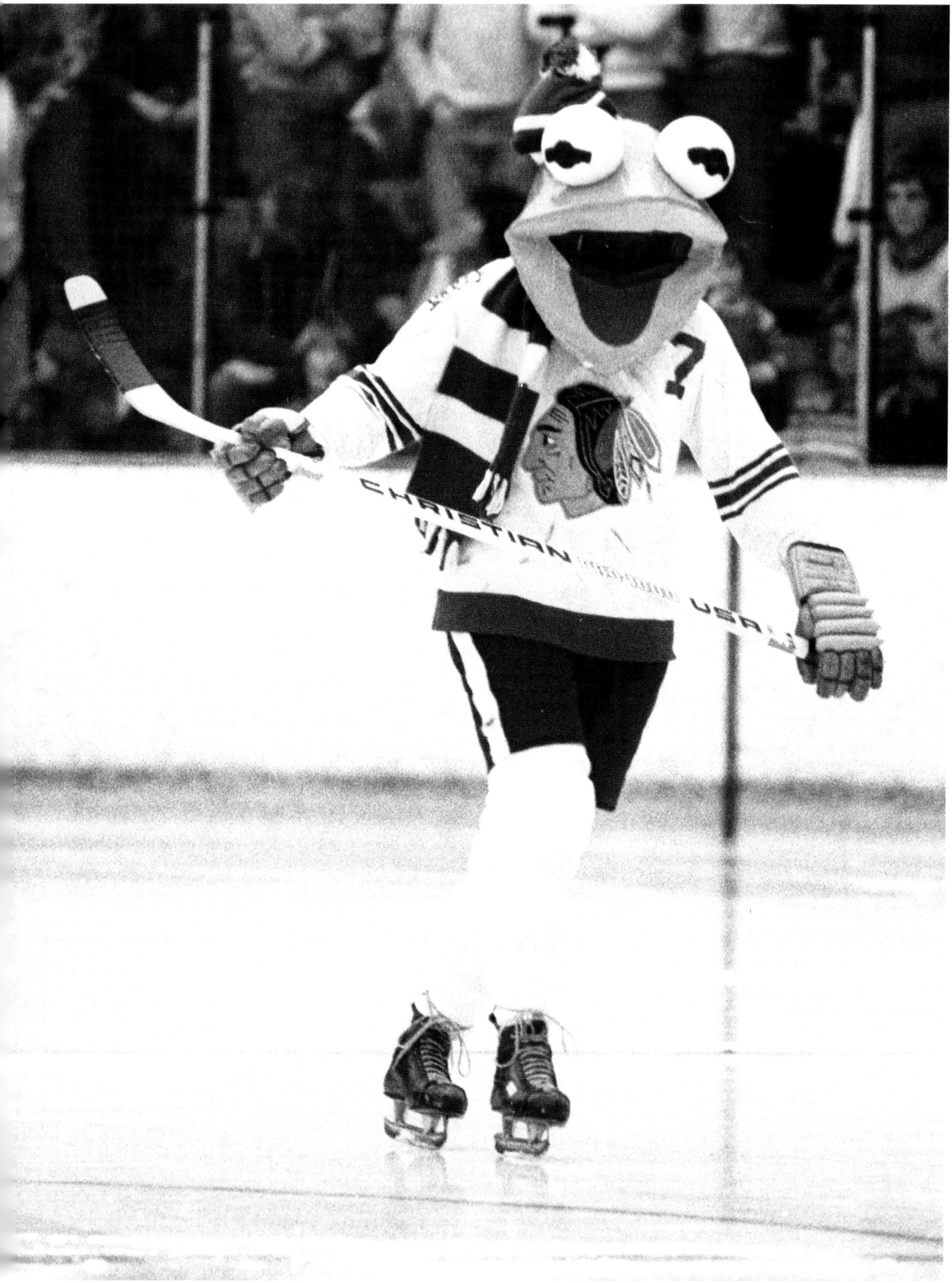
7
CHRISTIAN
USA

1979-1980 letterwinners

Frank Burggraf, *Roseau, Minn.*
Dusty Carroll, *Charlottetown, Prince Edward Island*
Paul Chadwick, *Williams Lake, B.C.*
Marc Chorney, *Thunder Bay, Ont.*
Brad Cox, *Lethbridge, Alta.*
Dean Dachyshyn, *Devon, Alta.*
Mel Donnelly, *Edmonton, Alta.*
Travis Dunn, *Winnipeg, Man.*
Cary Eades, *Burnaby, B.C.*
Glen Fester, *Vernon, B.C.*
Bob Iwabuchi, *Edmonton, Alta.*
Darren Jensen, *Creston, B.C.*
Pierre Lamoureux, *Fort Saskatchewan, Alta.*
Craig Ludwig, *Eagle River, Wis.*
Troy Magnuson, *Chanhassen, Minn.*
Erwin Martens, *Cartwright, Man.*
Conway Marvin, *Warroad, Minn.*
Rick Myers, *East Grand Forks, Minn.*
Mike Neitzke, *Detroit Lakes, Minn.*
Doug Smail, *Moose Jaw, Sask.*
Phil Sykes, *Dawson Creek, B.C.*
Mark Taylor, *Vancouver, B.C.*
Mickey Volcan, *Edmonton, Alta.*
Howard Walker, *Grande Prairie, Alta.*
Glen White, *Rosetown, Sask.*
Rick Zaparniuk, *Edmonton, Alta.*
Head coach: **Gino Gasparini**
Assistant coaches: **Rick Wilson, Jim Nelson**
Head trainer: **A.G. Edwards**
Equipment manager: **Dave Kamrowski**

said. "They were as good as they were because they had the capabilities of playing the game at a very high tempo, playing a puck control game or playing it very physical."

You could say that the Sioux of 1980 were born to be champions, given birth by the frustrations they felt in 1979.

That 1978-1979 season, Gasparini's first as head coach, the Sioux came out of nowhere to win the Western Collegiate Hockey Association regular-season title.

They beat the University of Minnesota 4-2 in the final game of the season in fabled Mariucci Arena in Minneapolis to clinch the outright title — David Christian's slap shot into an empty net in the closing seconds clinching the victory.

But a week later in Detroit, Mich., Minnesota freshman Neal Broten dove to tip a puck in the third period over Sioux goalie Bob Iwabuchi, who raced out of the net in an attempt to clear the puck. That goal by Broten, from Roseau, Minn., gave Minnesota a 4-2 lead in an eventual 4-3 Gopher triumph.

"I think our 1980 team was a direct extension of the 1979 team," Gasparini said. "But it was a very intense year for us, because we were picked to do what we did (win an NCAA championship). Sometimes being able to accomplish what you're expected to do is very difficult."

It was a team that was explosive offensively. Doug Smail's record eight shorthanded goals that season haven't been topped in Sioux history. Teamed with either Phil Sykes or Mark Taylor on the penalty-killing unit, they were a dangerous combination, racking up 17 shorthanded goals.

"They could play four against five and outplay most teams," Gasparini said. "They were that dynamic."

It was a team built with greyhounds such as Taylor, Smail and Sykes. It was a team featuring bruising defensive specialists such as Howard Walker, Craig Ludwig, Paul Chadwick, Dean Dachyshyn and Cary Eades, guys who combined talent with an even larger dose of intimidation. It was a team that featured rock-solid goaltending from rookie Darren Jensen and sophomore Iwabuchi.

"Every team has its own character, so to speak," Gasparini said. "This team could play any style, depending which side of the bed they got out of in the morning."

In Taylor, UND may have had the best college player in the country.

A year before the Hobey Baker Memorial Award came into existence in 1981, The Hockey News magazine of Toronto, Ont., named Taylor as the U.S. College Player of the Year.

Taylor, who still ranks second on UND's career scoring charts with 265 points, had 33 goals and a team-leading 92 points in the 1979-1980 season.

Goalie Bob Iwabuchi does the splits to make this save. Iwabuchi was a key member of UND's 1980 NCAA championship team. *(photo, John Stennes, Grand Forks Herald)*

Below: *Focus, focus! Sioux captain Mark Taylor has his attention directed on the puck in this 1980 game against Minnesota. (photo, Jeff Olson, Dakota Student)*

But he broke his collarbone early in the first period of the NCAA title game, an injury that would have crippled most teams.

Not this one. Gasparini double-shifted freshman Frank Burggraf as center on two lines, and the rest of the Sioux simply took their game to a new level.

None took it higher than Smail. In the title game, Smail scored the first three goals, as UND took a 3-0 lead into the third period. Phil Sykes, a walk-on at UND a year earlier, had a goal and four assists, figuring in on every Sioux goal.

UND outshot the Wildcats 45-22 overall and skated off with the title for head coach Gasparini and assistants Jim Nelson and Rick Wilson, all three former Sioux players.

It was a team the professionals liked, too. After the season, NHL teams signed Smail, Walker, Ludwig and freshman Mickey Volcan to contracts, all of them giving up their remaining college eligibility to pursue NHL dreams.

All four made it, Ludwig eventually winning Stanley Cup championships with both Montreal and Dallas.

But in 1980, they simply helped make the Sioux a team to remember.

**Mark Taylor, captain of the
1979-1980 Sioux team, was named
by The Hockey News as the
U.S. College Player of the Year in 1980.**

*The first Zamboni! Members of "The Farce" — as a group of UND students called
themselves — demonstrate their version of ice resurfacing. A bicycle, with a shovel on
the front and a guy with a watering can on the back, made for a perfect Zamboni.
(photo, Ron Smith, Grand Forks Herald)*

Opposite: *Nice to meet ya! UND's Dean Barsness, a mild-mannered man from Grand
Forks, N.D., exchanges pleasantries with a visiting goalie at Engelstad Arena. In 134
career games at UND from 1980 through 1984, Barsness was whistled for just 12
penalties. (photo, John Stennes, Grand Forks Herald)*

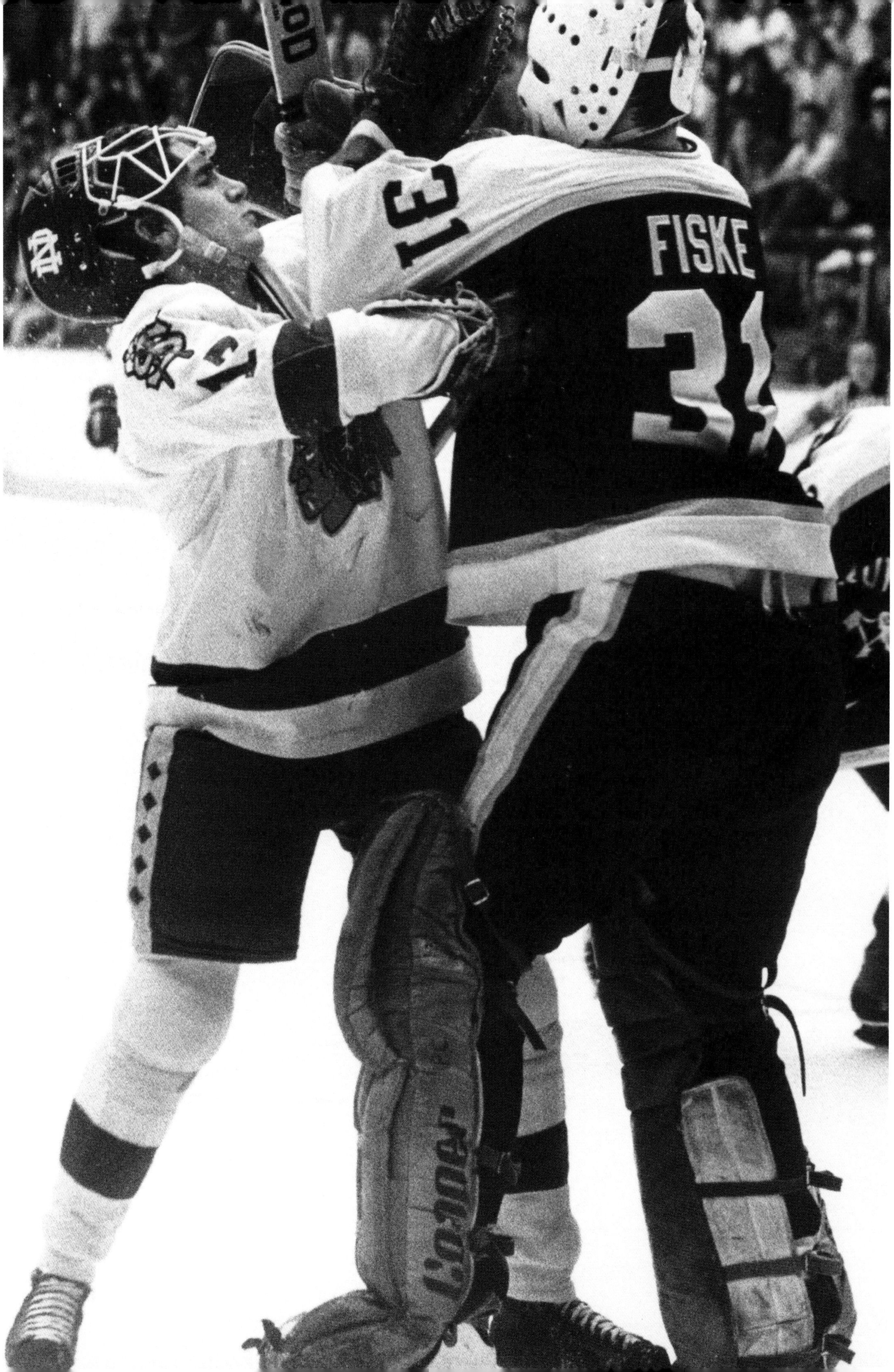
31
FISKE
31

1980

Providence Civic Center
Providence, R.I.
March 29, 1980

North Dakota 5, Northern Michigan 2

In John "Gino" Gasparini's second year as head coach, he wins the first of his three NCAA titles. After finishing second in the country in 1979, the Sioux make it to the top on March 29, 1980, in Providence, R.I. Four goals from Doug Smail, tournament Most Outstanding Player, lead the charge in a 5-2 championship victory over Northern Michigan. (photo, UND Athletics)

What happens when a team loses the best player in college hockey in the first period of a national championship game?

In the case of UND, it was a matter of regrouping, reloading and marching on.

Less than 10 minutes into the championship game, Mark Taylor left for good after breaking a collarbone on a collision. But before Taylor finished that shift, he teamed with Phil Sykes at 9:43 of the first period to set up the first of four goals by Doug Smail, putting the Sioux ahead to stay.

Taylor's injury would have crippled most teams. He scored 92 points that season and was named U.S. College Player of the Year by The Hockey News of Toronto, Ont., the year before the Hobey Baker Memorial Award came into being.

Taylor was checked hard at the Northern Michigan blue line, took several quick tumbles on the ice, then got up, dug out the puck from the corner and fired on net. Smail was there for the rebound. There was no stopping the Sioux after that.

The Sioux didn't learn until they returned to the dressing room after the first period that Taylor, a senior in his final game, would not return because of the injury.

"He said if we didn't go out and win the championship, he was going to beat the hell out of all of us with his good arm," said Sioux defenseman Marc Chorney, Taylor's roommate.

It was a bittersweet win in a way. "I'm happy we won, but I'm so sorry for Mark," Chorney said. "All year long, he talked about carrying the championship trophy around the rink. That's how he wanted to be remembered. And now, he was unable to do it."

Instead, his teammates did it for him, both in postgame celebration and with a dominating on-ice performance — giving coach Gino Gasparini the first of three NCAA titles he'd win at UND.

The Sioux outshot the Wildcats 45-22, gaining sweet revenge for two losses to Northern Michigan earlier in the year in Marquette, Mich.

UND built a 4-0 lead early in the third period before the Wildcats rallied with two goals before Smail's fourth goal of the game sealed the victory with 1:39 remaining.

In the title game, Sykes had a goal and four assists. Rookie goalie Darren Jensen finished with just 20 saves and ended his freshman season with an unbeaten record (13-0-1).

The title came over the Wildcats, who won the Central Collegiate Hockey Association title and finished with the best national record at 34-6-1, but were finished off by UND in the game that meant the most.

"It's hard not to cry," Smail said at the time. "I think this victory showed not only the class of the team, but of the coaches, too, from Gino on down. Everyone had a job to do, and they did it. We had to pick up the slack left by The King and we did it. There's no doubt that Mark (Taylor) is the king of this team," Smail said.

But even with the King gone, the Sioux were crowned as champs.

Semifinals

Finals

Northern Michigan 5-4

North Dakota 5-2

National champion

Cornell (16-13)

Providence, R.I.
March 28

Northern Michigan (33-5-1)

Providence, R.I.
March 29

North Dakota 4-1

North Dakota (29-8-1)

Providence, R.I.
March 27

Dartmouth (18-10-1)

Inside the game

Saves: North Dakota (Darren Jensen, 20); Northern Michigan (Steve Weeks, 40).
Total penalties: North Dakota 10 for 20 minutes; Northern Michigan 8 for 16 minutes.
Power plays: North Dakota 1 for 3; Northern Michigan 0 for 5.
Officials: Steve Dowling (referee), John Ricci (referee), Duane Markus (linesman).
Attendance: 5,811.

1st

Goals
1. ND, Doug Smail (Phil Sykes, Mark Taylor) 9:43 (pp); 2. ND, Smail (Sykes, Travis Dunn) 12:48.
Penalties
ND, Smail (holding) :58; ND, Brad Cox (hooking) 5:47; NM, Mike Mielke (roughing) 8:56; NM, Greg Tignanelli (roughing) 11:59; ND, Dean Dachyshyn (roughing) 11:59; ND, Paul Chadwick (slashing) 16:49; NM, Bill Joyce (slashing) 16:49; NM, Joyce (high sticking) 19:16.

2nd

Goals
3. ND, Smail (Sykes) 3:12.
Penalties
NM, Keith Hanson (high sticking) 2:45; ND, Frank Burggraf (slashing) 2:45; ND, Cox (hooking) 4:17; NM, Jeff Tascoff (elbowing) 4:17; ND, Rick Myers (roughing) 10:39; NM, Terry Houck (elbowing) 13:15; NM, Mielke (roughing) 15:14; ND, Burggraf (elbowing) 15:14; ND, Chadwick (elbowing) 18:11.

3rd

Goals
4. ND, Sykes (unassisted) 8:02; 5. NM, Joyce (Don Waddell, Tom Laidlaw) 14:29; 6. NM, Houck (Hanson, Jeff Pyle) 15:26; 7. ND, Smail (Sykes, Burggraf) 18:21.
Penalties
ND, Marc Chorney (high sticking) 12:26.

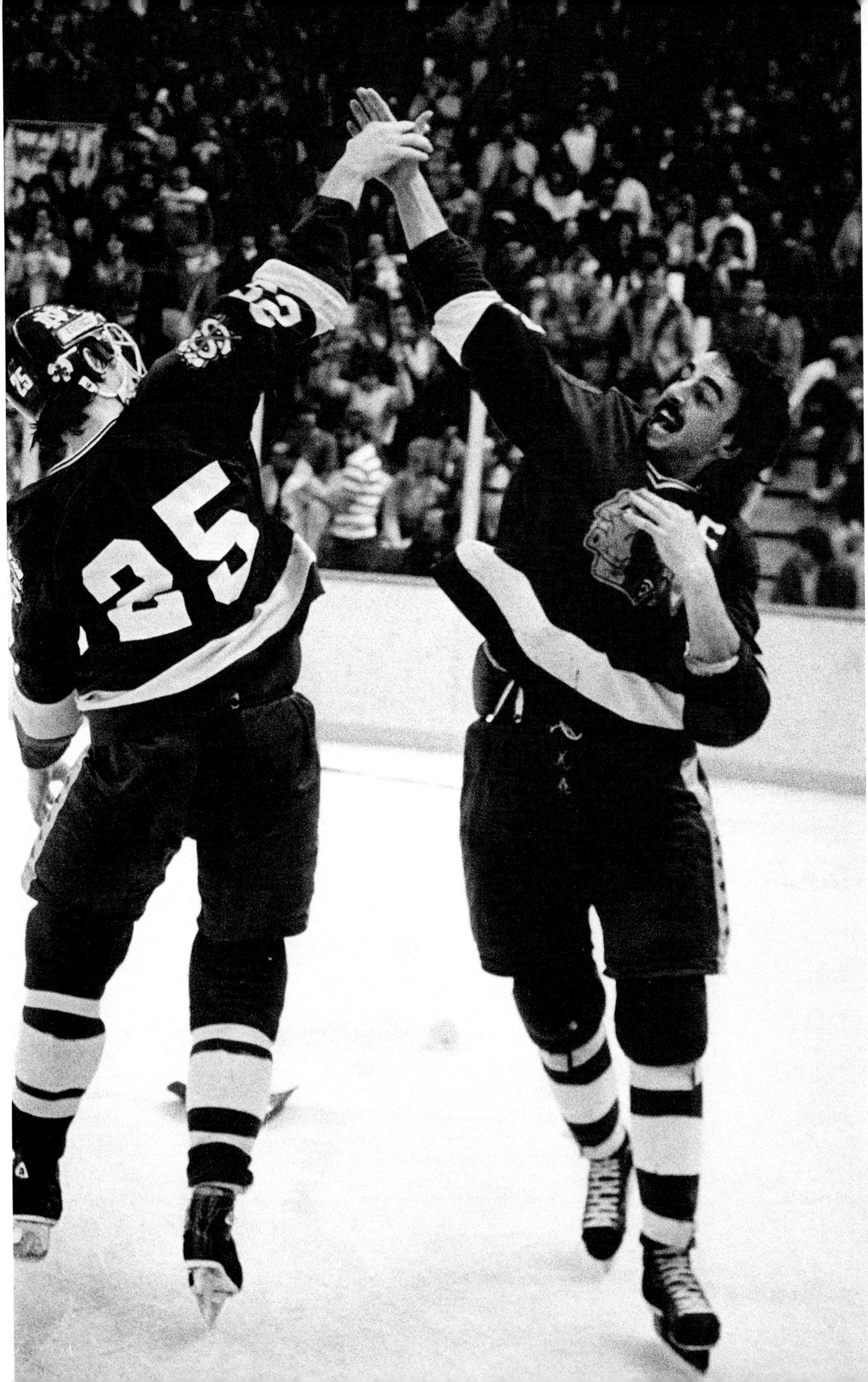

N o chapter on the NCAA championship won by the 1982 Fighting Sioux would be complete without a thorough understanding of conditions under which the title was won.

It came:

. . . During a four-year period when UND and Wisconsin alternated years as NCAA champions. The Sioux won in 1980 and 1982; the Badgers won in 1981 and 1983.

. . . When the gold medal won by the U.S. Olympic hockey team, a collection of mostly college players, spurred new interest in college hockey. The 1980 Olympic Games brought better players to college hockey and heightened the rivalries.

. . . When the national championship game might have featured the best collection of talent of any NCAA title game in history.

Between the Sioux (12 players) and Wisconsin (nine), a mind-boggling 21 players who battled in the 1982 title game in Providence, R.I., went on to play in the National Hockey League.

Two players from the championship game, UND's James Patrick (Buffalo) and Wisconsin's Chris Chelios (Detroit), still are active in the NHL, 20 years after an epic battle in Providence.

The 21 players have combined for nearly 10,000 games in the NHL or more than 500 a year since 1982. If you use the number of games played in the NHL as a barometer of talent, the 1982 championship game is a runaway winner for best in NCAA history.

UND sent Patrick, Craig Ludwig, Troy Murray, Dave Tippett, Rick Zombo, Phil Sykes, Jon Casey, Dave Donnelly, Gord Sherven, Darren Jensen, Jim Archibald and Dan Brennan from the Frozen Four title game in 1982 to the NHL.

From the University of Wisconsin came Chelios, Bruce Driver, Brian Mullen, Pat Flatley, Marc Behrend, John Newberry, Phil Houck, John Johannson and Terry Kleisinger.

Not only was this John "Gino" Gasparini's best team based on the

"There was absolute hatred between our teams. From top to bottom of the lineup, we despised them, and the feeling was mutual."

Cary Eades, Sioux winger

Opposite: You betcha! Phil Sykes (25) shares a high-five with fellow Sioux captain Cary Eades after the 1982 NCAA title game. Sykes had three goals and one assist in the 5-2 victory over Wisconsin to win tournament Most Outstanding Player honors. Eades scored UND's fourth goal. (photo, John Stennes, Grand Forks Herald)

1981-1982 letterwinners

Jim Archibald, *Craik, Sask.*
Dean Barsness, *Grand Forks, N.D.*
Dan Brennan, *Dawson Creek, B.C.*
Frank Burggraf, *Roseau, Minn.*
Dunstan "Dusty" Carroll,
Charlottetown, Prince Edward Island
Jon Casey, *Grand Rapids, Minn.*
Eddie Christian, *Warroad, Minn.*
Dean Dachyshyn, *Devon, Alta.*
Dave Donnelly, *Edmonton, Alta.*
Cary Eades, *Burnaby, B.C.*
Glen Fester, *Vernon, B.C.*
Darren Jensen, *Creston, B.C.*
Pierre Lamoureux, *Fort*
Saskatchewan, Alta.
Craig Ludwig, *Eagle River, Wis.*
Troy Magnuson, *Chanhassen, Minn.*
Troy Murray, *St. Albert, Alta.*
Arley Olson, *Eatonia, Sask.*
Steve Palmiscno, *Grand Forks, N.D.*
James Patrick, *Winnipeg, Man.*
Gord Sherven, *Mankota, Sask.*
Mike Stone, *Roseau, Minn.*
Phil Sykes, *Dawson Creek, B.C.*
Dave Tippett, *Prince Albert, Sask.*
Glen White, *Rosetown, Sask.*
Bill Whitsitt, *Bloomington, Minn.*
Rick Zombo, *Des Plaines, Ill.*
Head coach: **Gino Gasparini**
Assistant coaches: **Dean Blais**
and Don Boyd
Head trainer: **A.G. Edwards**
Equipment manager: **Dave**
Kamrowski

list of future professionals but one that stood out in his mind at the time, too.

"I remember commenting to someone at the time that this team was good enough to play in the Central Pro League," Gasparini said.

All six of Gasparini's freshmen recruits — Archibald, Sherven, Patrick, Zombo, Donnelly and Tippett — went on to play in the NHL. Has any college ever had a better rookie class?

Sykes, named the Most Outstanding Player in the 1982 tournament, scored 15 points in four NCAA tournament games over the 1980 and 1982 tournaments, both held in Providence.

"I sure was having fun in Providence," Sykes said. "It's hard for me to explain why that was."

In 1997, Sykes was named to the NCAA's 50th anniversary team. The team, chosen by coaches of teams who had participated in NCAA tournaments, featured 21 players. From UND, just Sykes and Tony Hrkac, the star of the 1987 championship team, were included.

"But it was never about me," Sykes said. "It was about us as a team, and the success we had in the national tournaments. That's the way it was then, and the way it still is today. We're still very close to each other. The bond has never been broken."

Sykes marvels how roles get reversed. He was such a star in 1982 that he was shadowed in the championship game by Wisconsin's Pat Flatley. But not very well, obviously.

Later in the NHL, Sykes shadowed Flatley when Flatley developed into a scoring star and Sykes became a noted defensive specialist.

While Gasparini had the highly acclaimed freshman class in 1982, it didn't feature the team leaders.

"Those freshmen were a big part of the puzzle," Gasparini said. "But the leaders of the team were guys like Sykes, Cary Eades and Craig Ludwig. They were the ones who made our team go and provided the leadership."

The Sioux had plenty of big-time players, too. "You have to have
players who rank in the top 5 percent of all the college players in the
country," Gasparini said. "You don't win championships unless you have
big-time players."

Gasparini had plenty of them.

"We had too many leaders and so many good players, I hate to even
mention them by name for fear that I'll forget someone," Gasparini said.

Gasparini knew he had great talent in 1982 and solid assistants
helping him coach with a youngster named Dean Blais and Don Boyd,
now director of scouting for the NHL's Columbus Blue Jackets.

Eades and Sykes were captains of the 1982 championship team.
Eades had missed the 1980 championship game after breaking an ankle in
a game at Wisconsin in midseason.

He wasn't about to let his last chance go by.

"I really sensed the urgency of doing everything possible to get that
championship," Eades said. "I remember having a lot of speeches in the
locker room between the second and third periods that season."

No victory meant more than the title game triumph over the
University of Wisconsin, UND's bitter rival.

53

Phil Sykes, the Most Outstanding Player in the 1982 tournament, was named to the 21-player NCAA 50th anniversary team in 1997, along with Tony Hrkac, a star on the 1987 title team.

"There was absolute hatred between our teams," Eades said. "From top to bottom of the lineup, we despised them, and the feeling was mutual. It was a war out there when we played Wisconsin."

Wisconsin fans had grown to hate Eades in particular, stemming from his active role in the infamous brawl in Madison's (Wis.) Dane County Coliseum that season.

Wisconsin fans would chant, "Eades is a goon, Eades is a goon," when he took the ice.

But when UND beat Wisconsin to claim the national title, Eades took the championship trophy, skated directly in front of the thousands of red-and-white-clad Badger fans and raised the trophy high.

What followed was one of the more memorable moments in college hockey.

The same Wisconsin fans who had grown to hate Eades — and the Sioux — rose as one and gave him (and the Sioux) a standing ovation.

"The relationship between the two schools and the two teams changed instantly at that moment," Eades said. "It had deteriorated to an all-time low after the brawl in Madison."

But in Providence in late March 1982, UND not only won a national title but the respect of its most hated opponent.

What could be better than that?

Opposite: Just call this double trouble. UND's Phil Sykes (right) and Cary Eades (left) combine to knock down Colorado College's Bruce Aikens in this game in Grand Forks, N.D. (photo, John Stennes, Grand Forks Herald)

Below: Here's to you. Teammates Conway Marvin, Travis Dunn and Mel Donnelly celebrate a national championship in 1980 with a refreshment. They were at the hotel in Providence, R.I., waiting for the bus to take the team to the airport for the return trip to Grand Forks. (photo, John Stennes, Grand Forks Herald)

1982

Providence Civic Center

Providence, R.I.

March 27, 1982

North Dakota 5, Wisconsin 2

UND gains sweet revenge on Wisconsin in the NCAA title game in Providence, R.I. The Sioux beat the Badgers 5-2 behind a hat trick, plus an assist, from Phil Sykes. Two weeks earlier, Wisconsin had humiliated UND by a combined 12-1 count in the two-game, total goals Western Collegiate Hockey Association playoff finals in Grand Forks, N.D. (photo, UND Athletics)

It came down to what equated to the seventh game of the World Series of college hockey to declare a champion.

UND's Fighting Sioux and Wisconsin's Badgers, who had split six previous meetings, met the seventh time in the last game of the collegiate season with a national title on the line.

Actually, it came down to the third period after the Sioux and the Badgers — two bitter rivals from the Western Collegiate Hockey Association — traded a goal apiece in both the first and second periods for a 2-all standoff.

Senior co-captain Phil Sykes, who had a five-point night in the 1980 NCAA championship game, stepped up again. He scored the game-winning goal at 6:27 of the third period for a 3-2 Sioux lead.

Cary Eades upped the ante to 4-2 at 10:07, then Sykes collected his hat trick at 15:08 for the final margin.

It capped a remarkable time in NCAA final games for Sykes. With his five-point game in 1980

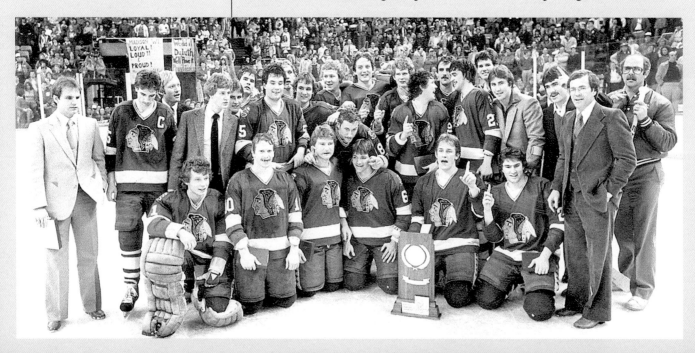

and a four-point game in 1982, Sykes finished with nine points in two NCAA title games spanning a three-year period.

UND outshot Wisconsin 38-25, with Darren Jensen backstopping the Sioux to a national title for a second time in a three-season span. He finished with 23 saves to 33 for Wisconsin's Terry Kleisinger.

Thanks to Sykes, the Big Red was dead. The title game hat trick was his third of the season against the Badgers.

"We wanted it so bad," Jensen said. "This makes me happier than even winning the 1980 title."

With regulars Dave Donnelly and David Tippett out with injuries, coach Gino Gasparini rolled three lines against Wisconsin's four, but the Badgers tired.

"We didn't want to get caught with any line mismatches; that's why I went with three lines,"

Gasparini said.

It helped that UND had a day of rest. The Sioux, who ripped Northeastern 6-2 on Thursday, rested and watched Wisconsin shut out New Hampshire 5-0 on Friday.

"The extra day of rest certainly helped us because of all our injuries," Gasparini said. "Down the last part of this season, we've been held together with blood, sweat and Band-Aids."

Gasparini devised a forechecking system that kept Wisconsin bottled up in its own end.

But Gasparini gave the credit to the players, not his system. "When it gets down to it, you can come up with any kind of system, but it doesn't do any good if you don't have the players to execute it," Gasparini said.

A pep talk by co-captain Eades, before the start of the third period, might have been a turning point, too.

"I told the guys that nobody remembers who takes second place in the nationals," Eades said. "I told them let's go out and win it, so we'll be a team to be remembered."

And so they are.

Sykes, a co-captain with Eades, was named the tournament's Most Outstanding Player. Joining him on the all-tournament team were teammates Craig Ludwig, a defenseman, and Eades.

Semifinals

Northeastern (24-8-2)

Finals

North Dakota 6-2

Providence, R.I.
March 25

North Dakota (31-12)

North Dakota 5-2

National champion

Providence, R.I.
March 27

Wisconsin (30-10-1)

Providence, R.I.
March 26

Wisconsin 5-0

New Hampshire (20-12)

Inside the game

Saves: North Dakota (Darren Jensen, 23); Wisconsin (Terry Kleisinger, 33).
Total penalties: 4 for 8 minutes; Wisconsin 5 for 10 minutes.
Power plays: North Dakota 0 for 4; Wisconsin 0 for 3.
Officials: Wayne Houmiel (referee), Dennis Parrish (referee), Terry Kirby (linesman).
Attendance: 9,272.

1st

Goals
1. ND, Glen White (Phil Sykes, Glen Fester) 1:26; 2. W, Ron Vincent (Tim Thomas) 3:56.
Penalties
W, Vincent (high sticking) 4:27; ND, Jim Archibald (roughing) 7:58; ND, Troy Murray (high sticking), 9:02.

2nd

Goals
3. ND, Sykes (Gord Sherven) 1:09; 4. W, John Newberry (Ted Pearson, Pat Flatley) 5:30.
Penalties
W, Chris Chelios (high sticking) 6:04; ND, Jim Patrick (tripping) 8:33; W, Pat Ethier (slashing) 16:16; W, Kleisinger (slashing, served by John Johannson) 17:05; ND, Sykes (slashing, served by Steve Palmiscno) 17:05.

3rd

Goals
5. ND, Sykes (Craig Ludwig, White) 6:27; 6. ND, Cary Eades (Murray, Dean Dachyshyn) 10:07; 7. ND, Sykes (White, Rick Zombo) 15:08.
Penalties
W, Chelios (hooking) 6:40.

The Hrkac Circus *1986-1987*

H as a team ever captured the imagination of college hockey fans across America more than the 1986-1987 Fighting Sioux?

This was a tremendous team, skilled and exciting. It included five players who went on to play in the National Hockey League, five who became All-Americans and the school's only Hobey Baker Memorial Award winner in Tony Hrkac.

No wonder a fan from East Grand Forks, Minn., came up with a name that went a long way toward insuring the fame of this team. Hilary Ryan, an East Grand Forks businessman, won a contest run by the Grand Forks Herald newspaper to name the line centered by Tony Hrkac.

His idea? The Hrkac Circus.

It rhymed, for starters (Hrkac rhymes with circus). Even though the name originally was designed to apply just to the Hrkac line, it caught on fast and was applied to the entire team. The Fighting Sioux of 1986-1987 became the Hrkac Circus.

Even today — some 15 years after that season — you'll find fans nationwide who'll make reference to the Hrkac Circus.

And what a show they put on under the big top of old Engelstad Arena. They rang up 40 victories, an NCAA record, and scored a Western Collegiate Hockey Association record 200 goals in 35 league games. That season, junior left wing Bob Joyce scored 52 goals, and sophomore center Hrkac scored 46 — still No. 1 and No. 2 in the UND single-season record books.

With 264 goals in 48 games, the 1986-1987 team stands as the highest-scoring unit in UND history, averaging 5.5 goals a game.

Yet, the Sioux entered the season as somewhat of an unknown, coming off a 24-16-1 record the year before and a sixth-place WCHA finish.

But two important steps took place. Hrkac decided to return to UND after a year's stint with the Canadian National team, and goalie Ed Belfour signed with the Sioux out of Carman, Man.

*A familiar sight in the 1986-1987 season featured Tony
Hrkac and Bob Joyce combining for a goal. Hrkac had
70 assists that season — still a school record — and
Joyce scored 52 goals, also a record. (photo, Eric Hylden,
Grand Forks Herald)*

"The two questions we had going into the season were who would take charge offensively and in goal," said Steve Johnson, a Grand Forks (N.D.) Central High School product who played on the Hrkac line for much of the season. "Those were our two big unknowns."

The unknowns turned into well-known players in a hurry. Belfour posted three shutouts, a .915 save percentage and a solid 2.43 goals-against average in 33 games.

And Hrkac? He set a national scoring record that stands today, highlighted by his 70-assist season.

Still, the season began with tragedy.

A car accident on Labor Day weekend north of Bemidji, Minn., took the life of incoming Sioux freshman George Pelawa, a 6-foot-4, 240-pound giant who was a No. 1 draft pick of the Calgary Flames.

"He had skated with us a few times when we were fooling around on our own," Sioux senior defenseman Tarek Howard said. "You could tell he was going to be something special."

The Sioux took a bus to Bemidji for the funeral. "It was a real sobering experience for a lot of guys," Howard said. "You realize you're not invincible."

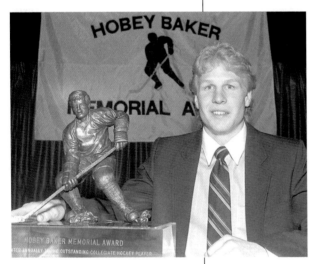

UND's only Hobey Baker Memorial Award winner, Tony Hrkac, accepts the trophy at the Decathlon Club in Minneapolis. Hrkac scored an NCAA record 116 points in the 1986-1987 season in leading the Sioux to the national championship. (photo, John Stennes, Grand Forks Herald)

Pelawa would have been a star. "There was no question but that George was going to play and play a lot," coach John "Gino" Gasparini said. "If I was going to write down line combinations before that season started, it would have been him on the right wing with Hrkac and Joyce. That would have been an interesting line."

The Sioux easily kept fans' interest.

"My most satisfying year of coaching at UND was my first year," Gasparini said. "The most coaching enjoyment came from the 1984 team, which finished third in the nation and went far beyond where I thought they could. The most fun year? It was 1987."

Yet it was a team with intensity, too. Belfour, even then, carried his game face through both practices and games. Ditto for forward Scott Dub, who played his heart out after coming in from tiny Pisek, N.D.

"Often, Monday practices after a weekend of games are pretty lame, without much intensity," Johnson said. "With Belfour and Dub in particular, they made sure that never happened. But the coaches had something to do with that, too."

No kidding? UND defenseman Ian Kidd can't believe what he's hearing out of the mouth of an Alaska Anchorage player in this game during the 1986-1987 season. Kidd, the only UND player ever from Oregon (Gresham), earned All-America honors as a sophomore that season but signed a pro contract when the season ended. (photo, Jackie Lorentz, Grand Forks Herald)

Said Howard: "With Gino, and John Marks and Dean Blais as the assistants, we were incredibly well-coached."

Gasparini said one of his biggest challenges in 1987 was getting his team to play to its talent level. "My biggest battle at times was motivating them," Gasparini said. "Like the 1980 team, this was a team that I thought had the capability to go undefeated."

It did not, but 40 wins were impressive.

However, the 1986-1987 Sioux struggled at times.

They lost to Michigan Tech, the last-place team in the WCHA that year. They lost at home to Colorado College and to U.S. International, a San Diego-based team coached by Brad Buetow in its first years of a brief fling with college hockey.

"There were certainly some games where we took the opponent for granted," Johnson said.

The return of Hrkac to UND was critical to the 1986-1987 success.

"I remember Tony telling me that playing for the Canadian National team was a wonderful experience," Gasparini said. "But he said it wasn't like playing for a league or a national title like in college. I thought that was an astute statement on his part."

Johnson, one of many former Sioux players who have gone into coaching after their days at UND, had his love for the game sharpened by UND's program.

"I think why you see so many former UND players in coaching is that you develop a real passion for the game once you go through the

Center Tony Hrkac and goalie Ed Belfour, both of whom earned All-America honors during UND's 1987 national championship season, helped the Dallas Stars of the NHL win the Stanley Cup in 1999.

Not this time. Sioux goalie Ed Belfour makes a sprawling save in UND's 1986-1987 championship season. When the season ended, he signed as a free agent with the Chicago Blackhawks. (photo, Jackie Lorentz, Grand Forks Herald)

Opposite page: *Was it the coaching or the talent? Either way, this was a pretty good combination in the 1986-1987 season. Tony Hrkac (left) led the nation in scoring, Bob Joyce (center) led the nation in goals and Gino Gasparini was national coach of the year. (photo, Eric Hylden, Grand Forks Herald)*

program," Johnson said. "If you're not a truly competitive hockey person at UND, you likely won't make it through the program."

This 1986-1987 team was competitive, from Belfour to Hrkac to Dub to Joyce to Johnson — right down the roster.

"But it was more than a collection of some very good players," Johnson said. "There was a camaraderie between the players that exists today."

Said Howard: "No matter whether they were freshmen or seniors, we all hung out together away from the rink. That never happened on other teams I was associated with."

Gasparini said the 1986-1987 Sioux were dynamic in all aspects of the game.

Following that season, sophomore defenseman Ian Kidd, freshman goalie Ed Belfour and forwards Bob Joyce, a junior, and Tony Hrkac, a sophomore, all gave up their final years of eligibility to sign pro contracts.

"Sometimes I look back and wonder that if everything was in a Utopian situation and they had all stayed in school, how many national titles we could have put together," Gasparini said.

Gasparini said he taught tough love to his players, no different than parenting, he said.

Hrkac, suspended as a freshman at UND by Gasparini, took a year off, came back and led one of the greatest college teams in history to national glory.

It's that kind of story that Gasparini cherishes far more than the victories behind his name or the fact that he won 392 games at UND, more than any other coach in school history.

"When winning and losing supersedes your principles and ethics," Gasparini said, "it's time to get out of the business."

Gasparini coached seven more seasons at UND after the 1986-1987 season of glory but never again reached that level of success.

Sioux defenseman Russ Parent keeps a Yale University player tied up in this scuffle during the 1986-1987 season in Grand Forks, N.D. Linesman Buzz Olson (left) does his best to keep peace in the game won 6-4 by the Sioux. (photo, Eric Hylden, Grand Forks Herald)

Oops! UND's Lee Davidson (14) knocks Denver University's Jay Moore sideways with this high stick in a 1989 game in Grand Forks, N.D. Davidson had 202 points in his career from 1986 through 1990. (photo, Jackie Lorentz, Grand Forks Herald)

1987

Joe Louis Arena
Detroit, Mich.
March 28, 1987

North Dakota 5, Michigan State 3

UND sets a school record for wins (40), as John "Gino" Gasparini picks up his third and last NCAA title as Sioux coach. On March 28, 1987, at Joe Louis Arena in Detroit, Mich., the Sioux beat Michigan State 5-3 to claim the school's fifth NCAA title. Tony Hrkac, named as the Hobey Baker Memorial Award winner during the tournament, is the tournament Most Outstanding Player. (photo, UND Athletics)

The Grand Forks (N.D.) Herald, in a special section devoted to the 1987 NCAA tournament, labeled this tournament as the Showdown in Motown.

If you're going to put on a show, what better act to bring than the fabled Hrkac Circus?

The Tony Hrkac-led Fighting Sioux picked up their NCAA-record 40th victory by winning the title, rolling over Michigan State from the Central Collegiate Hockey Association.

The Sioux, 20 strong in this 40th annual NCAA tournament, put in a solid 60 minutes to win UND's fifth national title.

UND took command early, building a 3-0 lead in the first period with a burst of three goals in a span of one minute and 55 seconds.

With all the attention focused up front on such prolific Sioux scorers as Hrkac, Bob Joyce and Steve Johnson, defensemen stole the show early on.

Ian Kidd backhanded in a

feed from Joyce for the opening goal at 15:07, and Murray Baron, a rookie, skated in alone from his defensive spot to slip a shot past MSU goalie Bob Essensa at 16:44 for a 2-0 lead.

Before the Spartans could recover, Joyce slapped in a centering pass from Hrkac 18 seconds later against the shell-shocked Spartans.

"We dug ourselves a real hole early and as good of a team as North Dakota is," Michigan State coach Ron Mason said, "it's very tough to come back."

With rookie Ed Belfour in goal for the Sioux, Michigan State never had much of a chance. Belfour, who gave up just 2.4 goals a game in his lone season with the Sioux, was solid.

Tom Tilley beat Belfour early in the second period, chopping UND's lead to 3-1. But Mal Parks answered that seven minutes later for a 4-1 cushion.

Kevin Miller tried to rally Michigan State with his goal late in the second period, but it was answered by Brent Bobyck's breakaway goal at 7:54 of the third period for a 5-2 lead.

Kip Miller, Kevin Miller's brother, scored the final goal for the Spartans.

It was the third — and last — title won under coach Gino Gasparini.

"This was as sweet as the last one (in 1982), maybe better than most, because of all the records this team set," Gasparini said.

Hrkac capped a personal hat trick of awards after the title game on Saturday by being named Most Outstanding Player in the NCAA tournament. On Thursday, he was named to the All-America team and,

on Friday, he won the Hobey Baker Memorial Award.

"Winning the championship is my biggest thrill," he said. "And having five different players score goals shows the depth of this team."

It did indeed. It might have been called the Hrkac Circus in 1987, but clearly the Sioux had a lot of showstoppers.

Contributions came from everyone in the title game, not just the highly acclaimed Hrkac.

"There were no stars on this team tonight," said Joyce, the team captain. "It's an honor for me to be captain of a bunch of guys like this. I just hope I've done them justice."

Semifinals
Minnesota (33-13-1)

Finals
Michigan State 5-3

Detroit, Mich.
March 27
Michigan State (32-9-2)

North Dakota 5-3
National champion

Detroit, Mich.
March 28

North Dakota (38-8)

Detroit, Mich.
March 26
Harvard (28-4)

North Dakota 5-2

Inside the game

Saves: North Dakota (Ed Belfour, 15); Michigan State (Bob Essensa,18).
Total penalties: North Dakota 5 for 10 minutes; Michigan State 6 for 12 minutes.
Power plays: North Dakota 1 for 5; Michigan State 0 for 4.
Officials: Pierre Belanger (referee), Rod Christensen (linesman), Steve Piotrowski (linesman).
Attendance: 16,632.

1st
Goals
1. ND, Ian Kidd (Bob Joyce) 15:07 (pp); 2. ND, Murray Baron (Jeff Bowen, Kidd) 16:44; 3. ND, Joyce (Kidd, Tony Hrkac) 17:02.
Penalties
MS, Tom Tilley (hooking) 1:05; ND, Grant Paranica (holding) 7:09; MS, Brad Hamilton (tripping) 12:45; MS, Danton Cole (tripping) 13:54; ND, Tom Benson (high sticking) 18:06.

2nd
Goals
4. MS, Tilley (Brian McReynolds, Mitch Messier) 8:30; 5. ND, Malcolm Parks (Scott Koberinski) 15:05; 6. MS, Kevin Miller (unassisted) 16:56.
Penalties
ND, Scott Dub (slashing) 3:16; MS, Hamilton (tripping) 3:57; MS, Sean Clement (hooking) 9:53; ND, Baron (cross checking) 12:55.

3rd
Goals
7. ND, Brent Bobyck (Russ Parent) 7:54; 8. MS, Kip Miller (Ke. Miller) 18:34.
Penalties
MS, Don Gibson (late hit) 12:07; ND, Lee Davidson (roughing) 12:07.

Dean Blais (right) and John "Gino" Gasparini share some good times, perhaps rehashing a previous victory over those pesky University of Minnesota Gophers. Blais worked as Gasparini's top assistant from 1980 through the 1988-1989 season. (photo, Eric Hylden, Grand Forks Herald)

Blais-ing a trail *1994-2001*

Dean Blais has built a national reputation as one of college hockey's great coaches.

Yet, as with most successful coaches, he's a blend of men he's played for or coached under, including former UND coach John "Gino" Gasparini.

"Gino gave me the opportunity to come here," said Blais, who served as an assistant under Gasparini from 1980 to 1989.

It turns out to be one of the best recruits Gasparini ever landed.

Since replacing Gasparini as head coach in 1994, most notable of Blais' achievements have been the two national titles in 1997 and 2000. That's in addition to four of the last five Western Collegiate Hockey Association championships through the 2000-2001 season.

A two-time winner of the Spencer Penrose Award as national coach of the year, it hasn't taken Blais long to rebuild UND's program to the level of glory the Sioux rose to under Gasparini in the 1980s.

UND associate coach Dave Hakstol said the perception is out there that Blais wrings the absolute most out of his teams.

He's a demanding coach, Hakstol said, but he's far more than that.

"Respect is a huge factor," Hakstol said. "The kids like playing for him, and they have fun playing for him. He's tough with discipline. The players know where that line is — and they don't cross it."

Hakstol played at UND when Gasparini was the head coach, and he now coaches under Blais. "One key thing they have in common is that they both demand excellence," Hakstol said.

Blais has won at a record pace. UND's three straight WCHA titles from 1997 through 1999 tied the league record for consecutive crowns. The current streak of four WCHA titles in five years never had been done before.

The man who runs it all for the Sioux is a Minnesota Golden Gopher, of all things. Yes, he's a product of UND's greatest rival. Blais skated for the Gophers from 1969 to 1973 under the coaching of Glen

"The dream of mine isn't to coach in the National Hockey League. I'm living my dream right here — with the right team."

Coach Dean Blais

Sonmor for three seasons and Herb Brooks for one.

He learned from Gasparini, Sonmor, Brooks, Bob Johnson and many others, including the legendary Larry Ross, his coach at International Falls (Minn.) High School.

"I've been very lucky to have good coaches all the way through," Blais said.

"Sprinkle in my experiences with USA Hockey (with National, Junior and Olympic teams) and that gave me a lot of international experience and a lot of experience of dealing with different players from different parts of the country and the world," Blais said.

In contrast to Gasparini, Blais gives more control and responsibility to his assistant coaches, Hakstol and Brad Berry.

"It's nice to have a small say in what goes on," Hakstol said. "But Dean controls the ship. In the end, Dean makes the decisions."

When daughter Mary Beth became ill in December 2000 and required extensive care, Blais named Hakstol as associate head coach, responsible for the Sioux program in his absence.

It was a supreme vote of confidence toward a first-year assistant. It echoes Blais' belief that UND's hockey program is the nation's best, top to bottom.

From the coaching staff to the medical staff to the equipment staff to the secretary to the Zamboni driver, Blais said no school in the nation has a better staff.

Preparing the Sioux for their trip to yet another NCAA tournament, coach Dean Blais finds time for a light moment and a good chuckle with a caller wishing the Sioux and Blais well. (photo, John Stennes, Grand Forks Herald)

But he almost didn't end up at UND.

In 1980, Blais had the choice of returning to the University of Minnesota as an assistant coach under Brad Buetow or coming to UND as Gasparini's assistant, replacing Rick Wilson.

"I think I chose the right program for me," Blais said.

Though Minnesota is his alma mater, he became close to UND while coaching high school hockey in Minot, N.D. During the summers, he worked the UND hockey schools. He wanted to get his master's degree in education as well, and that opportunity was open to him at UND.

He learned early on the importance of discipline on a team.

"You have to have it not only on the ice but off the ice," Blais said. "Players have to go to class and do the job there, too."

In that light, he instituted a program of monitoring classes his players are enrolled in. If there's an unexcused absence, the offending player runs the steps at Engelstad Arena at 6 a.m. "Education by intimidation," Blais says, with his usual hearty laugh.

His players have been aces both on the ice and in the classroom, generally with a team average above 3.0 (a B grade). "You recruit good students, but if there's a player out there like a Travis Roche who can

70

It's a family reunion. At the 2001 NCAA Frozen Four in Albany, N.Y., coach Dean Blais visits at the Pepsi Center with his father, Bill, and his son, Ben, who came out to watch the Sioux practice. (photo, John Stennes, Grand Forks Herald)

Dean Blais has been named WCHA coach of the year three times — in 1997, 1998 and 2001 — and has won the Spencer Penrose Award as national coach of the year twice — in 1997 and 2001.

win you a national championship," Blais said, "you take him. You can't have all 3.0 students on your team."

Blais said he's changed as a coach over the years, perhaps more than the players have. After all, he said, when Herb Brooks coached the Pittsburgh Penguins, he didn't try to tell all-stars Mario Lemieux or Jaromir Jagr how to play. "You don't compromise your thoughts, you just try different approaches to get them across," Blais said. "I think that's what I've learned to do — to have a different approach with the players."

Blais acknowledges that the level of the talent pool isn't as deep as it was in the early 1980s.

But you can do more with less sometimes, too. "I think what we've done is get a lot out of average players," Blais said. "I think you see that our players get better in this program."

He cites players such as Jeff Panzer, Lee Goren, Bryan Lundbohm and Mike Commodore, who all struggled somewhat as freshmen but left UND with NHL contracts in hand.

"I think that's noted around the country now, that the players get better here," Blais said. "I think that has to do with not only the coaches but our entire staff. There isn't a weak link in our organization."

Yet it all goes back to the enthusiasm and dedication Blais possesses for Sioux hockey. He'll drive any distance, through any storm, to scout and recruit.

When those prospects become Sioux players, Blais is there as a hands-on coach to develop them. "I love practice," Blais said. "I'm a fundamentals coach. Gino Gasparini was a great analyst, strategist and tactician, and he had to be with the talented players he had. Now, no college

has that talent level."

To his credit, Blais didn't skip a beat when longtime assistant and close friend Scott Sandelin left UND to become head coach at the University of Minnesota-Duluth.

He brought in Hakstol, a former Sioux player, former pro and a longtime head coach in the United States Hockey League with great recruiting contacts in the prime development league for college players.

And he brought in former UND player Brad Berry, an ex-NHL defenseman. Berry, who has a variety of recruiting contacts in Canada and around the world, replaced Jeff Bowen.

Blais clearly has proven to be a man who can adjust. When Olympic-size rinks became the vogue around the WCHA, Blais brought in smaller, quicker players to combat the larger ice surface. It's a strategy that worked so well that his 1997 championship team used the phrase "Speed Kills."

He was forced to go with smaller, skilled players in part, too, because the first batch of bigger, stronger players he sought chose other schools over UND and the school's unknown coach — Blais.

"You talk to those kids now, and right down the line, they'll tell you they should have gone to North Dakota," Blais says today of those players. "The rings, the watches, the championships, the notoriety, the improvement, they missed all that by not coming here."

Blais returned to UND in 1994 after leaving in 1989 to coach Roseau (Minn.) High School, where he guided the Rams to a Minnesota state championship in his first season as coach. He also coached two years in International Falls, Minn., his hometown.

The brain trust of Sioux hockey. Head coach Dean Blais and first-year assistant coaches Brad Berry (left) and Dave Hakstol (right) evaluate the players during a scrimmage late in the 2000-2001 season. (photo, John Stennes, Grand Forks Herald)

Opposite: *At the 2000 NCAA tournament in Providence, R.I., friends and rivals talk before the tournament opens as Maine coach Shawn Walsh visits with Dean Blais. UND beat Maine 2-0 in that tournament on its way to its seventh NCAA championship. When Walsh was diagnosed with cancer later in 2000, the next season Blais and the Sioux donated a set of UND jerseys to Maine for auction. The jerseys brought in more than $10,000 to help Walsh and others in hockey with cancer. (photo, Eric Hylden, Grand Forks Herald)*

"I had to establish myself as being a head coach," Blais said of his reasons for going from college to high school. "I thought the best way to do that was to go back to high school. I wasn't going to get a head college job without that step. I had chances at St. Cloud (Minn.) State and Colorado College (in Colorado Springs), and I was in the top three."

He wasn't No. 1, though. But in 1994, he had the chance to return to UND. He was UND athletic director Terry Wanless' selection to replace Gasparini.

Blais' secret for success? "I think it has a lot to do with fundamentals," Blais said. "When the players hit the ice, we're going to work hard, have fun — and improve our talent level."

Blais has an instinct for the game. "You've got to have a gut feeling in certain situations," he said. "When you've been around like I have, you know what it takes."

Beginning with the start of the 2001-2002 season, he enters the third year of his five-year contract at UND. After the 2003-2004 season ends,

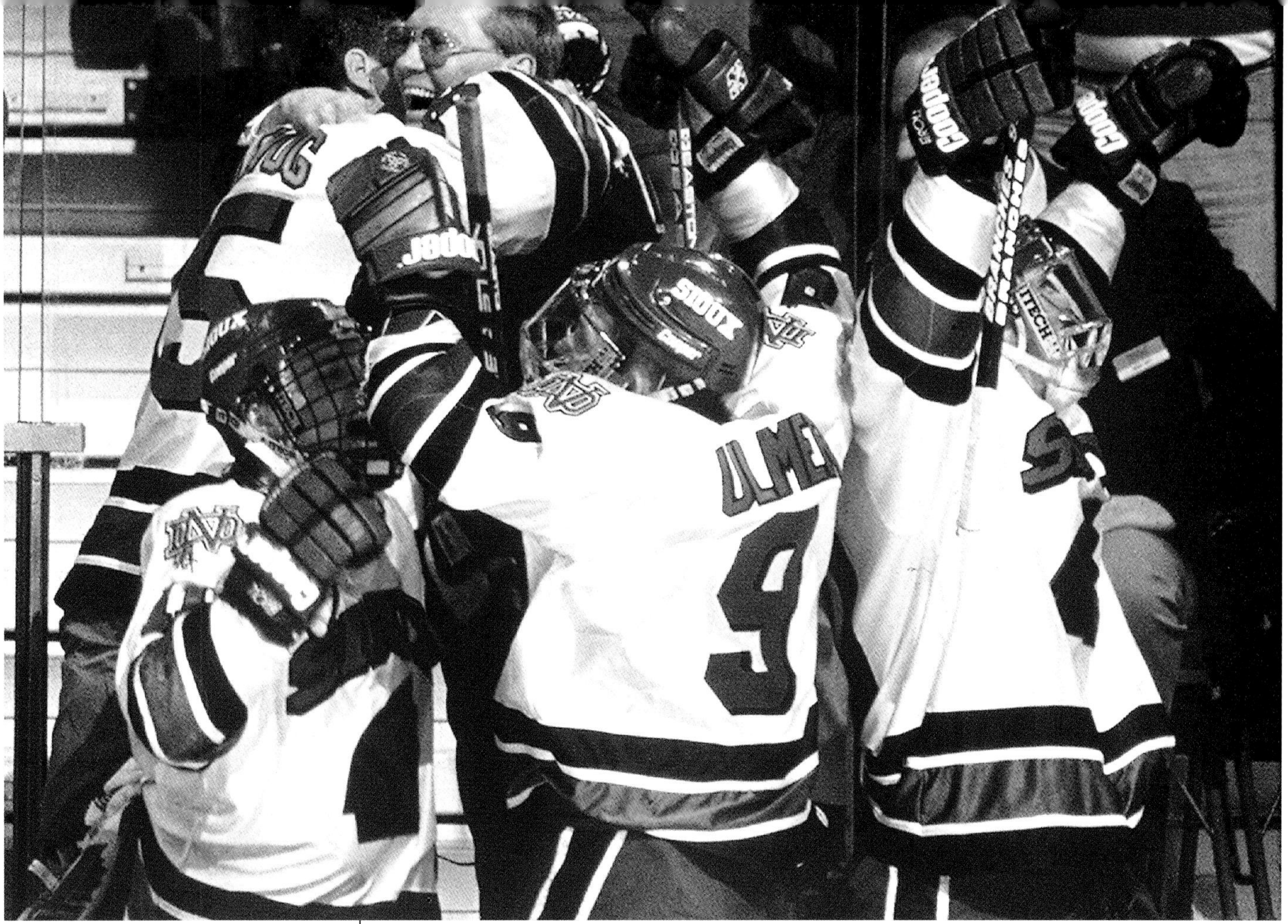

So sweet! Dean Blais gets a hug from reserve goalie Toby Kvalevog as the Sioux clinch the 1997 NCAA Frozen Four championship in the Bradley Center in Milwaukee, Wis. (photo, Tom Lynn)

he'll be eligible for the full $500,000 annuity set up for him by UND when he signed his five-year contract.

How much longer he'll stay at UND is uncertain. "I hope that it'll be forever," Hakstol said.

That won't happen, though.

Blais said he'll review his situation when his contract is up and decide if he wants to stay or try something else.

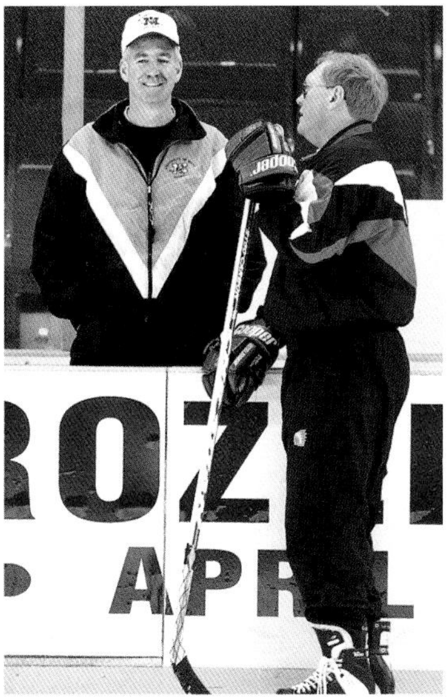

He's a small-town boy who loves a smaller city, such as Grand Forks, where excellent hunting and fishing — two of his passions — are just a short drive away.

"I can't stand, for example, the drive from Lakeville (Minn.) to downtown Minneapolis, through all the traffic," he said. "A big city isn't for me. But if the right opportunity came along, even next year ... ."

It's not so much about money, Blais said. Lifestyle ranks high with him, and he's comfortable here.

He interviewed for the head coaching jobs of two NHL expansion teams, the Minnesota Wild and Columbus Blue Jackets, in the summer of 2000, but others were chosen.

"The dream of mine isn't to coach in the National Hockey League," Blais said. "I'm living my dream right here — with the right team."

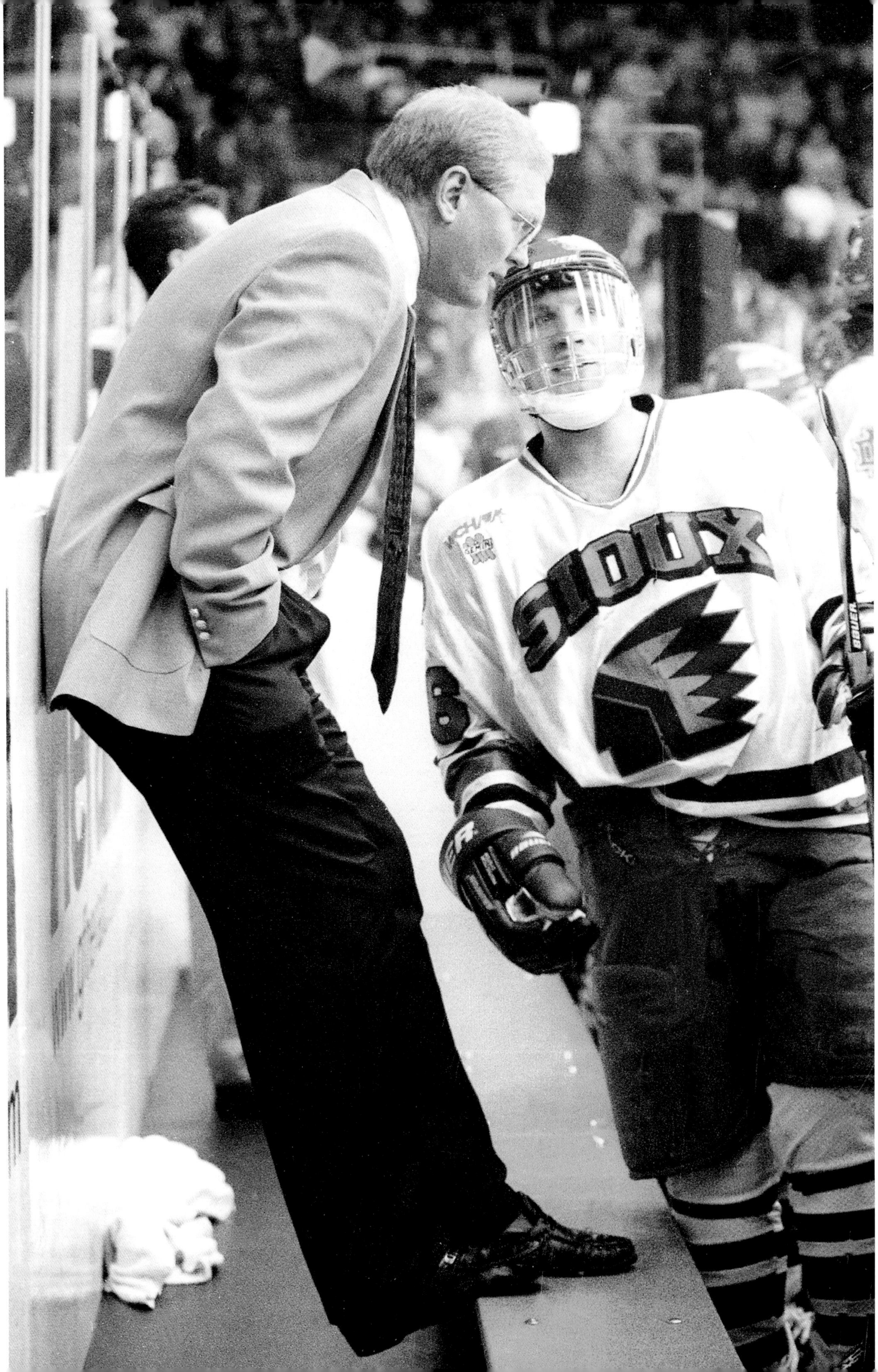
SIOUX

Opposite: Coach Dean Blais and Jay Panzer hold a conversation along the bench in Engelstad Arena. Panzer, from Grand Forks, N.D., was a key member of UND's 1997 NCAA title team. (photo, John Stennes, Grand Forks Herald)

At the Providence (R.I.) Civic Center in 2000, Dean Blais celebrates a goal of his own during a shooting competition the Sioux usually hold once a week. Maybe it was a setup job, but Blais beat out his players in this game to win it all, just like his players did later in the Frozen Four there. (photo, Eric Hylden, Grand Forks Herald)

All for one *1996-1997*

UND's 1997 national championship team will be remembered as much for a senior goalie who stepped aside as it will be for the freshman goalie who stepped up and carried it to the title.

Toby Kvalevog, a senior goalie from Bemidji, Minn., and a regular for three seasons, relinquished his No. 1 role to rookie Aaron Schweitzer from Regina, Sask., halfway through the season.

That unselfish move paid big dividends for the Sioux, who won 19 of their 25 games once the calendar flipped to the year 1997. Included was a 7-0 run through the league, regional and national tournaments.

"What won it for us was Schweitzer taking over the goaltending right around Christmastime," UND coach Dean Blais said. "He was the difference in winning the national championship."

While Schweitzer posted a 17-3 win-loss record, a 2.31 goals-against average and a .908 save percentage, the willingness of Kvalevog to turn from starter to teacher was just as important to the success.

"The neat thing about Toby when Aaron took over his place is that Toby helped Aaron out," Blais said. "Toby coached him. Toby was the one who stayed after practice and really worked with Aaron."

Today, Kvalevog still is involved in hockey — as a teacher and a coach. "Maybe that was a real strength of his," Blais said. "He found that out at a time that was tough on him. Goalies are often temperamental, but Toby was unique in that he was willing to turn it over to a freshman with no bitterness. He was a true example of a real team guy. It's something I'll never forget."

This team caught everybody by surprise, including itself. It might have been one of the youngest teams to win a national title, with 13 freshmen and sophomores playing in the championship game.

The title came in Blais' third year as coach — and his first trip to the nationals.

"Everything was so new for us, since we hadn't won anything before," Blais said. "Then we won the WCHA, the league playoffs and

"We were sitting up there in the stands, and we knew we had a good chance once Boston University beat Michigan."

Coach Dean Blais

Opposite: Jeff Ulmer holds the championship trophy high and proud after doing his bit to help the Fighting Sioux win the NCAA Frozen Four title in the Bradley Center in Milwaukee, Wis. The Wilcox, Sask., native was one of two Ulmer brothers on the 1997 national championship team — younger Jason Ulmer being the other. (photo, Jeff Phelps, Milwaukee Journal Sentinel)

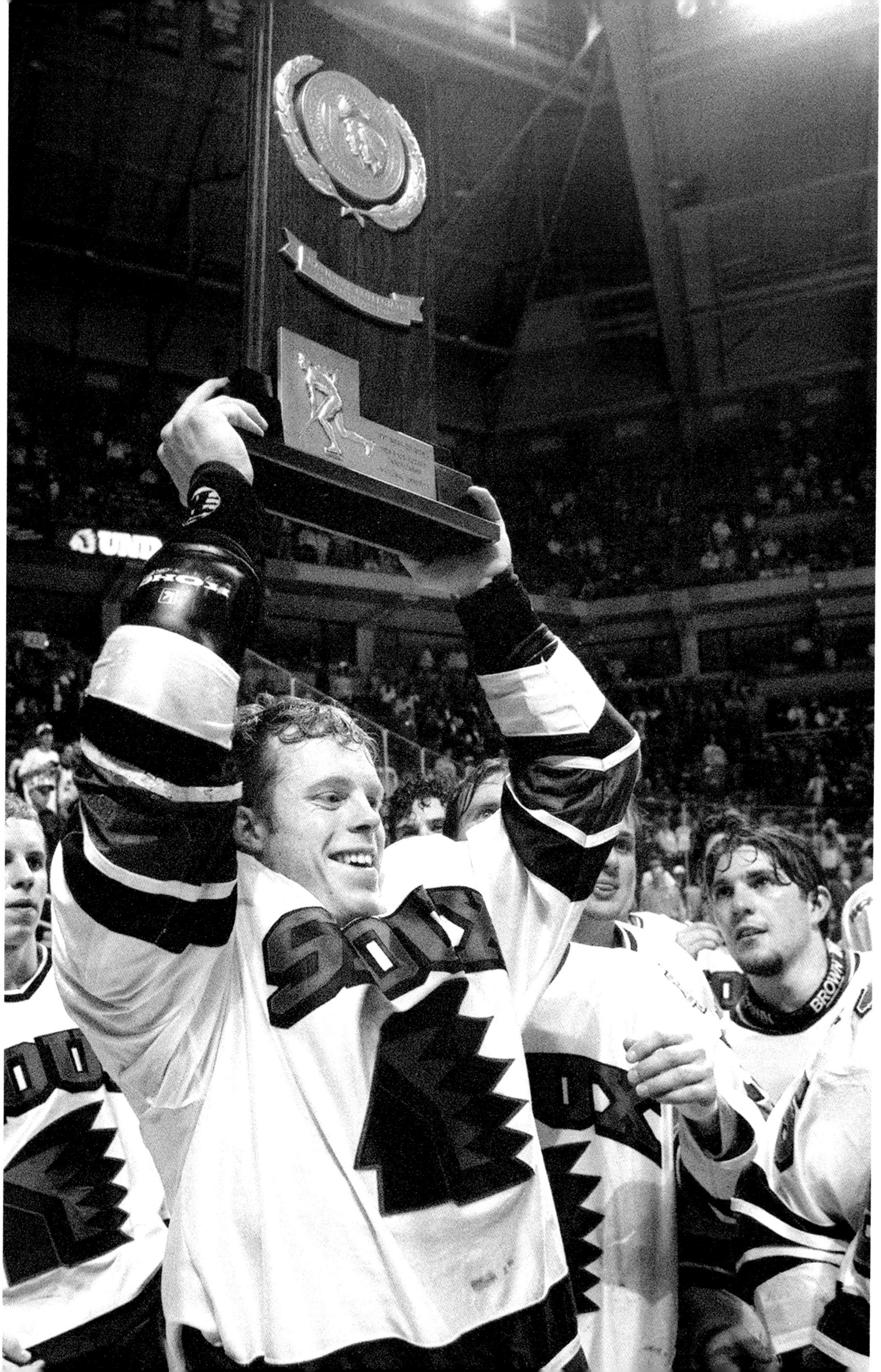
BROWN

1996-1997 letterwinners

Peter Armbrust, *Edina, Minn.*

Jason Blake, *Moorhead, Minn.*

Joe Blake, *Champlin, Minn.*

Jesse Bull, *Faribault, Minn.*

Adam Calder, *Portage la Prairie, Man.*

Brad DeFauw, *Apple Valley, Minn.*

Matt Henderson, *White Bear Lake, Minn.*

David Hoogsteen, *Thunder Bay, Ont.*

Kevin Hoogsteen, *Thunder Bay, Ont.*

Ian Kallay, *Whitecourt, Alta.*

Toby Kvalevog, *Bemidji, Minn.*

Dane Litke, *Beausejour, Man.*

Curtis Murphy, *Kerrobert, Sask.*

Tim O'Connell, *Grand Forks, N.D.*

Jay Panzer, *Grand Forks, N.D.*

Tom Philion, *Minot, N.D.*

Mark Pivetz, *Edmonton, Alta.*

Tyler Rice, *Winnipeg, Man.*

Aaron Schweitzer, *Regina, Sask.*

Jason Ulmer, *Wilcox, Sask.*

Jeff Ulmer, *Wilcox, Sask.*

Aaron Vickar, *St. Louis, Mo.*

Mitch Vig, *Bismarck, N.D.*

Brad Williamson, *Thunder Bay, Ont.*

Head coach: **Dean Blais**

Assistant coaches: **Mark Osiecki and Scott Sandelin**

Head trainer: **Mark Poolman**

Equipment manager: **Mike Schepp**

the national championship. While everything was new, we had the talent to do it."

Even in the national tournament in Milwaukee, Wis., UND was hardly the favorite. That role belonged to top-ranked University of Michigan, which had steamrolled through the Central Collegiate Hockey Association and was thought to be invincible.

But in the semifinals, the Wolverines were stunned 3-2 by Boston University. In the other semifinal, UND beat Colorado College 6-2. It was UND's fourth victory over the potent Tigers — who had won the previous three WCHA MacNaughton Cup titles — in six meetings.

"We were sitting up there in the stands, and we knew we had a good chance once Boston University beat Michigan," Blais said.

The Sioux turned "chance" into golden opportunity, thanks in part to a player from White Bear Lake, Minn. Matt Henderson walked on at UND without a scholarship in Blais' first year as coach in 1994 and became the outstanding player in the 1997 tournament.

All he did in two tournament games in Milwaukee was accumulate five points, including three goals, two of them in the title game.

Blais said he knew at the start of the year that this team could be something special. "We had great leadership — Dane Litke, Kevin Hoogsteen and Mark Pivetz as captains — and we had all those sophomores who were coming off a pretty good freshman season," Blais said.

A hug, anyone? Freshman goalie Aaron Schweitzer races out of the net in search of teammates moments after the Sioux clinch the 1997 NCAA championship in Milwaukee, Wis., with a 6-4 victory over Boston (Mass.) University. Schweitzer, from Regina, Sask., had five shutouts in the two seasons he played at UND. (photo, Jeff Phelps, Milwaukee Journal Sentinel)

Opposite: Sioux captain Dane Litke, a defenseman from Beausejour, Man., signals UND's status in the final game of the 1997 college season. With the scoreboard at the Bradley Center in Milwaukee, Wis., showing the results, Litke's smile says it all. (photo, Jeff Phelps, Milwaukee Journal Sentinel)

Yet the Sioux tied for the WCHA title with the University of Minnesota, UND losing two games to close the WCHA regular-season schedule at Denver University and allowing the Gophers to share the MacNaughton Cup.

But while the Sioux and the Gophers split four regular-season meetings, UND outscored Minnesota 20-19 in those games. It was the slimmest of margins — but a huge one.

It gave the Sioux the No. 1 seed in the league playoffs — and the last line change.

That last change paid off. In the WCHA Final Five championship game, Sioux freshman Peter Armbrust came off the bench on the line change. He picked up a puck shot by David Hoogsteen and put it into an open net for a 4-3 overtime victory.

That win locked up the No. 2 seed in the West Regional for the Sioux, who beat Cornell University 6-2 to advance to the Frozen Four.

Blais got big performances from many in the nationals. His so-called checking line of Henderson, Adam Calder and Jeff Ulmer had a hand in eight goals in the WCHA and NCAA playoff games — and didn't allow their opposing line to score.

A guy who played youth hockey in Grand Forks and wanted to come back home made a big difference, too.

That would be Jason Blake, who spent his freshman season at Ferris State of Michigan, then transferred to UND and sat out a year under the transfer rule.

"He made everyone better," Blais said.

UND wing Brad DeFauw (20) takes apart a Boston University player behind the net during the 1997 NCAA championship game. Sioux defenseman Mark Pivetz (3) moves in to pick up the pieces. (photo, Jeff Phelps, Milwaukee Journal Sentinel)

Matt Henderson, named the Most Outstanding Player in the 1997 NCAA tournament, originally came to UND without a scholarship as a walk-on from White Bear Lake, Minn.

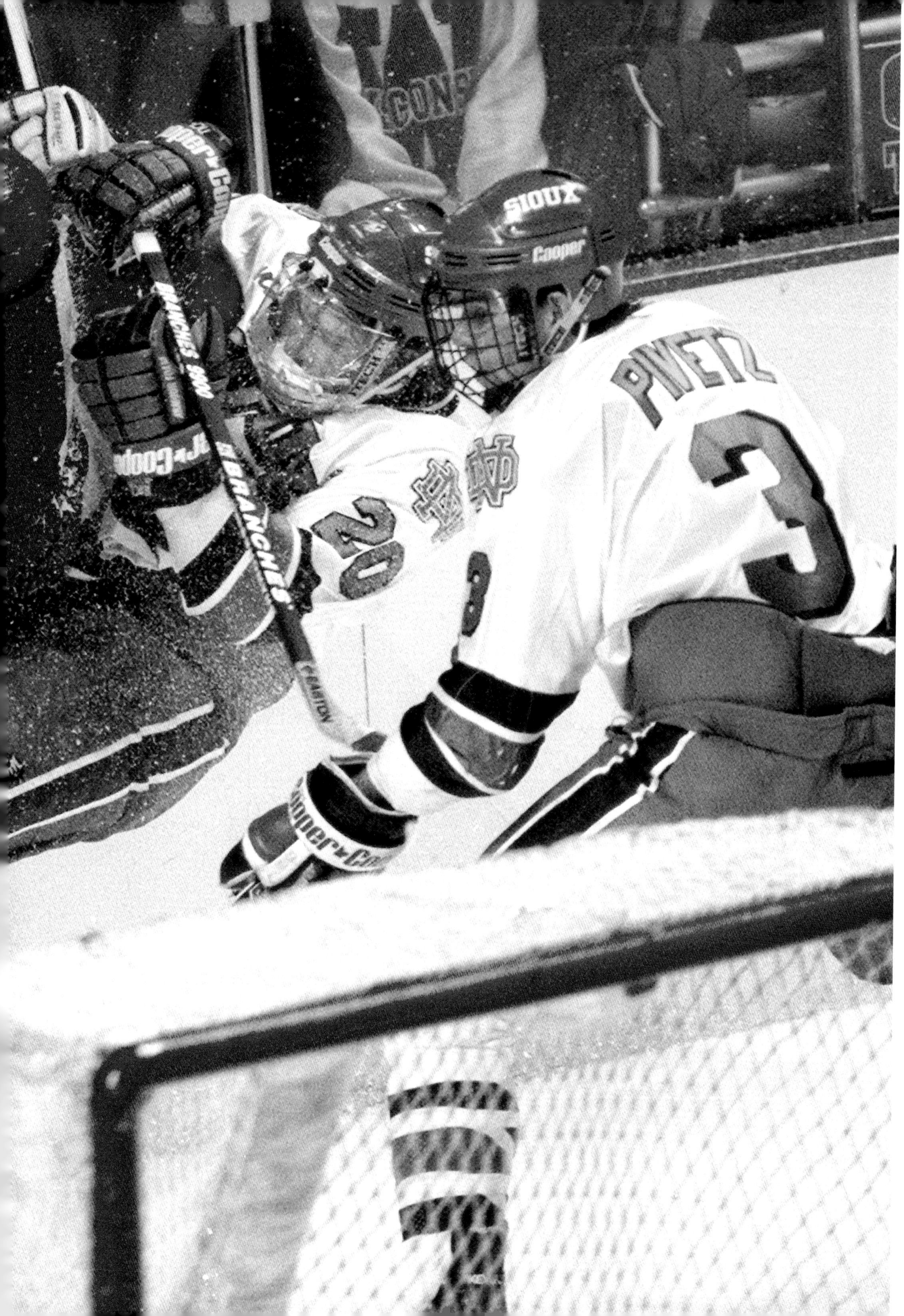
SIOUX
Cooper
PIVETZ
3
20
BRANCHES

In his first year at UND in 1996-1997, the former Moorhead (Minn.) High School standout led the team in assists and lived his dream of playing at UND and winning a national championship. He teamed with 5-foot-6 David Hoogsteen (27 goals, 27 assists) to form a dynamic pair of little speedsters. Blake added 51 points to finish No. 2 in scoring behind Hoogsteen.

Even so, Blais said there never was a point during the season when he felt UND would win the national title, simply because of all the other good teams out there — including Michigan and Boston University.

Against Boston in the title game, not even a 2-0 deficit after one period fazed the Sioux.

"I remember going into the dressing room, and the guys weren't panicking or anything," Blais said. "We didn't have to shock them, because we were playing fairly well."

The shock waves ran through the BU Terriers instead, when the Sioux exploded for five second-period goals.

Boston coach Jack Parker could offer only his congratulations. "My hat is off to the Fighting Sioux of North Dakota and especially to coach Dean Blais, who is a class act and a real gentleman of this game. They had a great win," Parker said.

Then Parker gave the ultimate salute to the Sioux. "I do believe the best team just won the national championship," Parker said. "because they took advantage of our disintegration — and made it even worse for us."

Not a single Sioux made the All-America team that season, though David Hoogsteen, Jason Blake and defenseman Curtis Murphy were all-WCHA selections.

"We had a lot of players with great character," Blais said.

And when it all ended in Milwaukee, a great championship as well.

Frozen Four Most Outstanding Player Matt Henderson (22) prepares to join the pile atop Sioux goalie Aaron Schweitzer after UND's victory in the 1997 NCAA Frozen Four title game. (photo, Jeff Phelps, Milwaukee Journal Sentinel)

Opposite: *A large turnout of Sioux fans are on hand in 1997 in Milwaukee, Wis., to cheer on UND to the national championship. The Sioux didn't disappoint the fans, beating Colorado College and then Boston (Mass.) University to bring home UND's sixth national title. (photo, Tom Lynn)*

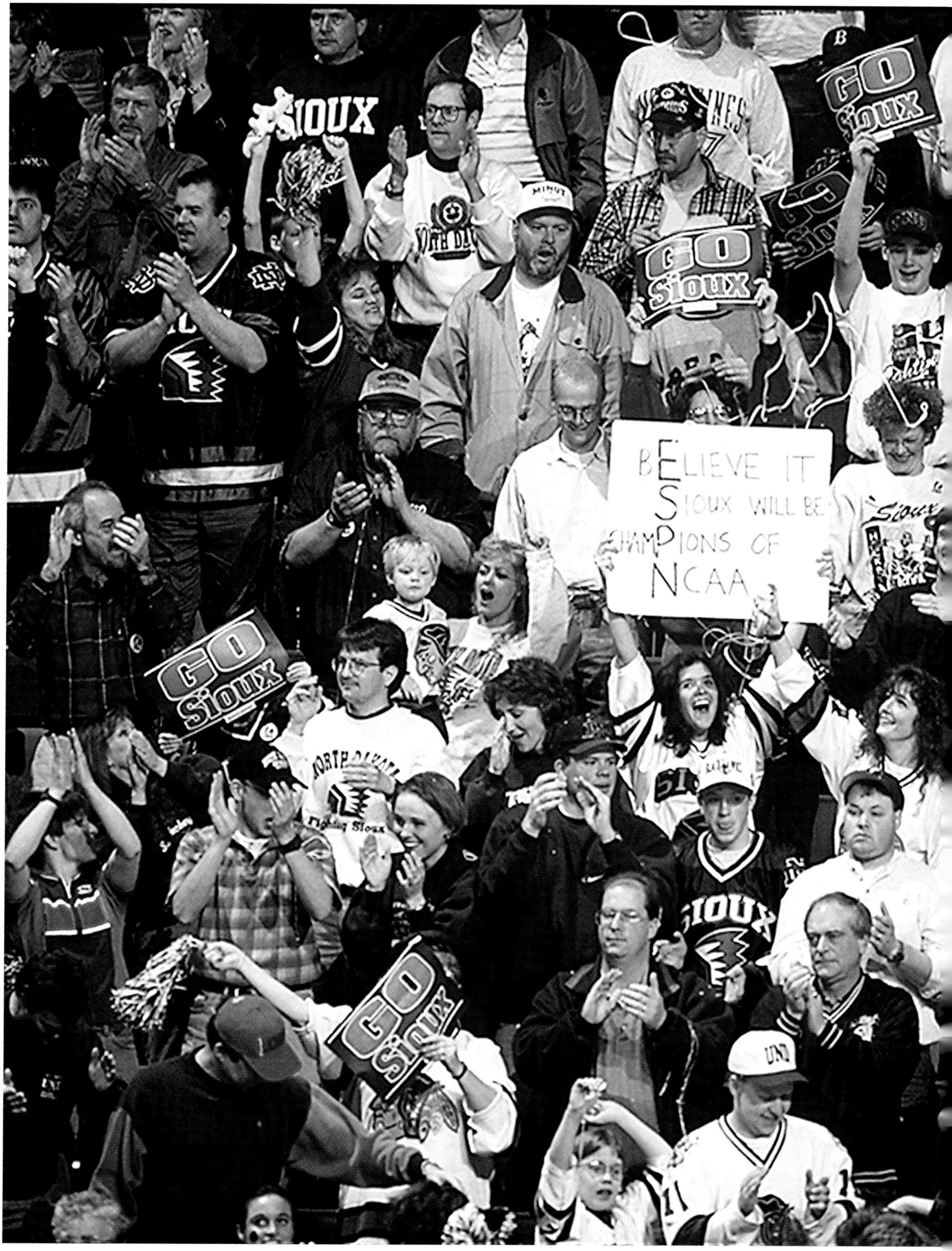
SIOUX
GO Sioux
bELIEVE IT
SIOUX WILL BE
CHAMPIONS OF
NCAA
GO Sioux
NORTH DAKOTA
Fighting Sioux
SIOUX
GO Sioux
UND

1997

Bradley Center
Milwaukee, Wis.
March 29, 1997

North Dakota 6, Boston University 4

In the NCAA title game on March 29, 1997, in the Bradley Center in Milwaukee, Wis., the Sioux get a lot of big performances. Matt Henderson, tournament Most Outstanding Player, and David Hoogsteen score two goals apiece as the Sioux roar back from an early 2-0 deficit to beat Boston (Mass.) University 6-4 for the championship. (photo, UND Athletics)

UND's players, referred to as "smurfs" at one point during the season by Western Collegiate Hockey Association commissioner Bruce McLeod, turned in a giant of a performance in the title game.

The Sioux, down 2-0 after one period, blitzed Boston (Mass.) University for five goals in the second period on their way to victory in front of 17,557 fans, the second-largest crowd to watch an NCAA championship game.

The smallest of UND's "smurfs," 5-foot-6, 140-pound David Hoogsteen, scored two goals in the second period to set up one of the most improbable championships in school history.

The Sioux, picked to finish fifth in the WCHA, completed a 7-0 run through the league and NCAA playoffs by taking apart Boston University, making its eighth-straight NCAA tournament appearance.

"We all knew we had a great bunch of guys," Hoogsteen said. "It

was just a matter of putting it together. We might not have the most talented team in the nation, but we have a lot of heart and determination. I think that's why we won."

Junior defenseman Curtis Murphy got the Sioux rolling in the second period. His goal from the right point at 7:06 of the period chopped Boston University's 2-0 lead in half.

Hoogsteen scored his first goal at 8:38 to tie it at 2-2, and Matt Henderson put the Sioux ahead to stay at 12:35 with his shorthanded, breakaway goal with Murphy in the penalty box.

Chris Kelleher's power-play goal brought Boston University even at 3-3 at 13:56.

But the Terriers' hopes vanished faster than Hoogsteen's flying feet.

Henderson answered Kelleher's power-play goal with one of his own at 15:49, giving the Sioux the lead for good at 4-3.

Then, with just six seconds left in the period, Hoogsteen broke Boston University's heart. He capped a furious Sioux attack, ramming in a loose puck just before the period horn sounded for a 5-3 lead.

UND then turned defensive, limiting Boston University to eight shots in the final period. Defenseman Jon Coleman scored with 36 seconds left in the game to make it 5-4, creating some anxious moments for the Sioux faithful.

But Adam Calder's empty-net goal with 13 seconds left ended the scoring and closed the chapter on how the

"smurfs" won a national title.

"We lost our composure and turned it over to a team that can absolutely, positively jump on those type of turnovers," Boston coach Jack Parker lamented. "I thought the goal at the end of the second period (by Hoogsteen) was the real crusher."

Henderson, who had come to UND as a walk-on in 1994, was named the tournament's Most Outstanding Player, with three goals and two assists in two games.

Hoogsteen, Murphy and goalie Aaron Schweitzer (25 saves) joined Henderson on the all-tournament team.

Semifinals

Colorado College (25-14-4)

Milwaukee, Wis.
March 27

North Dakota (29-10-2)

Finals

North Dakota 6-2

Boston University (25-8-6)

Milwaukee, Wis.
March 27

Michigan (34-3-4)

North Dakota 6-4

National champion

Milwaukee, Wis.
March 29

Boston University 3-2

Inside the game

Saves: North Dakota (Aaron Schweitzer, 25); Boston University (Michel Larocque,24).
Total penalties: North Dakota 6 for 12 minutes; Boston University 5 for 10 minutes.
Power plays: North Dakota 1 for 5; Boston University 2 for 6.
Officials: Matt Shegos (referee), John Dobrzelewski (assistant referee), John LaDuke (assistant referee).
Attendance: 17,537.

1st

Goals
1. BU, Peter Donatelli (Tom Poti) 8:44; 2. BU, Chris Drury (Poti, Albie O'Connell) 15:08 (pp).

Penalties
ND, Jesse Bull (hooking) 2:12; BU, Bill Pierce (interference) 4:47; BU, Chris Kelleher (interference) 9:40; ND, Matt Henderson (elbowing) 13:34.

2nd

Goals
3. ND, Curtis Murphy (Jay Panzer, Henderson) 7:06; 4. ND, David Hoogsteen (unassisted) 8:38; 5. ND, Henderson (unassisted) 12:35 (sh); 6. BU, Kelleher (unassisted) 13:56 (pp); 7. ND, Henderson (Adam Calder, Dane Litke) 15:49 (pp); 8. ND, Hoogsteen (Murphy) 19:54.

Penalties
BU, Greg Quebec (interference) 3:01; ND, Murphy (tripping) 11:44; ND, Mark Pivetz (interference) 13:12; BU, Matt Wright (interference) 15:02.

3rd

Goals
9. BU, Jon Coleman (Kelleher, Mike Sylvia) 19:24; 10. ND, Calder (unassisted) 19:47 (en).

Penalties
BU, Sylvia (cross checking) 8:02; ND, Mitch Vig (holding) 11:44; ND, Henderson (interference) 17:09.

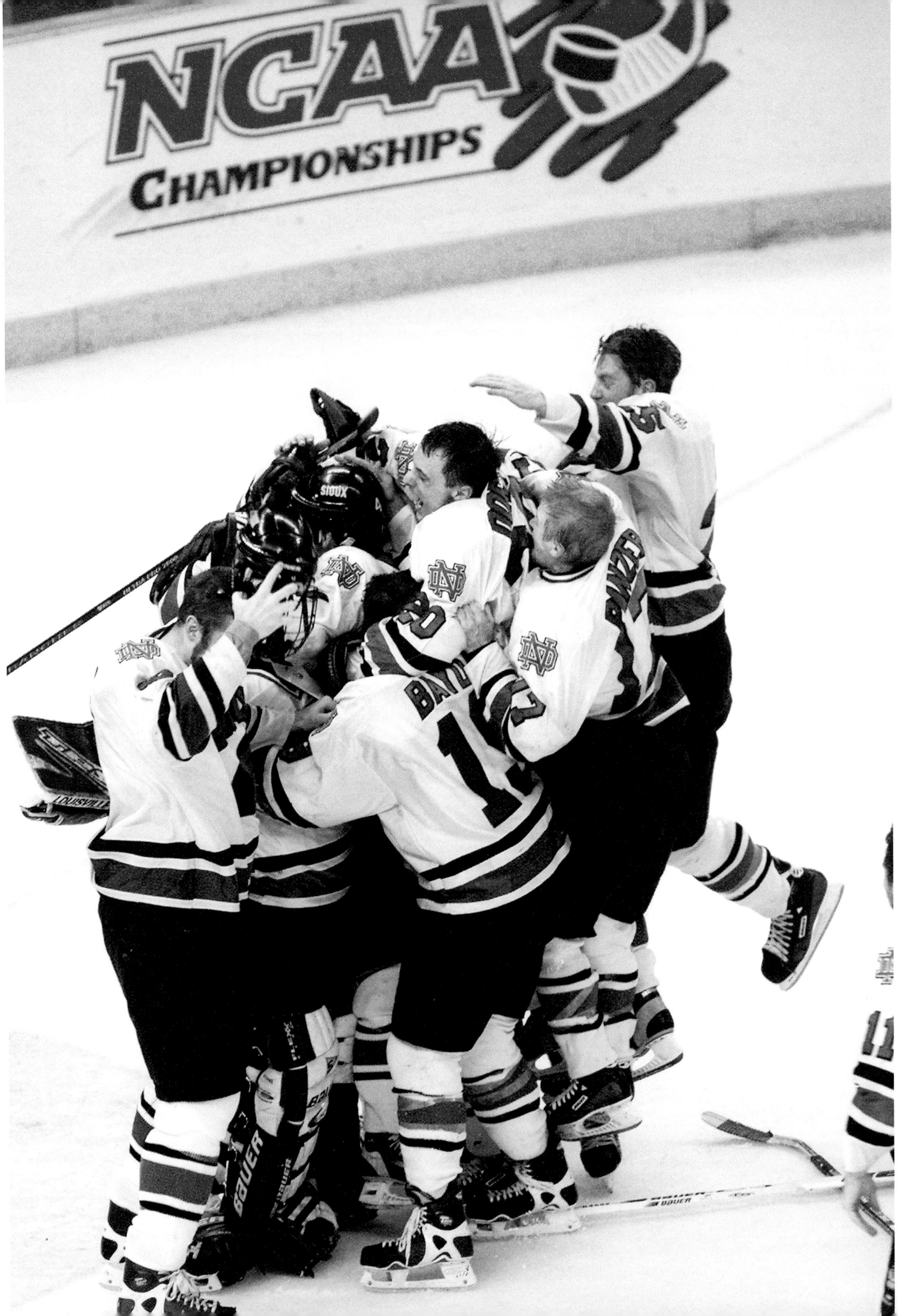
NCAA
CHAMPIONSHIPS

True grit and destiny *1999-2000*

Opposite: Seconds after the 2000 NCAA championship game ends on April 8 in Providence, R.I., Sioux players swarm goalie Karl Goehring to celebrate the 4-2 victory over Boston (Mass.) College and UND's seventh national hockey championship. (photo, Eric Hylden, Grand Forks Herald)

I n the history of UND hockey, only twice has a group of players won a national title as freshmen and seniors.

That's what happened to the 2000 senior class, which followed its first title in 1997 as freshmen with the ultimate graduation present as seniors.

Peter Armbrust, Brad DeFauw, Tim O'Connell and Jason Ulmer were the four who were part of championship teams in Milwaukee, Wis., in 1997 and in Providence, R.I., in 2000.

"We can talk about all the players underneath them," said UND coach Dean Blais, "but certainly it was the seniors who brought everything together."

The seniors joined some rather select company. Only the group of Frank Burggraf, Dusty Carroll, Dean Dachyshyn, Cary Eades, Glen Fester, Darren Jensen, Pierre Lamoureux, Craig Ludwig, Troy Magnuson, Phil Sykes and Glen White can match them in title rings. They all played on NCAA title teams under Gino Gasparini in 1980 and 1982.

The 2000 championship came on the heels of disappointments in 1998 and 1999. The Sioux teams of those years were perhaps talented enough to win NCAA titles but were upset in regionals to lower-seeded teams.

This was a team with special grit, though.

Despite a brilliant season of goaltending from junior Karl Goehring — eight shutouts, 1.89 goals-against average and .927 save percentage — UND still finished second in the WCHA to the University of Wisconsin. That snapped the record-tying string of three straight MacNaughton Cups for the Sioux.

But once the playoffs came about, the Sioux — not the Badgers — ruled.

UND defeated Wisconsin 5-3 for the WCHA playoff championship in Minneapolis and advanced through the NCAA West Regional, also in

1999-2000 letterwinners

Peter Armbrust, *Edina, Minn.*
Ryan Bayda, *Saskatoon, Sask.*
Mike Commodore, *Fort Saskatchewan, Alta.*
Brad DeFauw, *Apple Valley, Minn.*
Wes Dorey, *Edmonton, Alta.*
Jason Endres, *Grand Forks, N.D.*
Karl Goehring, *Apple Valley, Minn.*
Lee Goren, *Winnipeg, Man.*
Ryan Hale, *Colorado Springs, Colo.*
Trevor Hammer, *Roseau, Minn.*
Adrian Hasbargen, *Warroad, Minn.*
Pat Kenny, *Edmonton, Alta.*
Andy Kollar, *Winnipeg, Man.*
Chris Leinweber, *Calgary, Alta.*
Bryan Lundbohm, *Roseau, Minn.*
Chad Mazurak, *Regina, Sask.*
Paul Murphy, *Manvel, N.D.*
Jason Notermann, *Rochester, Minn.*
Tim O'Connell, *Grand Forks, N.D.*
Jeff Panzer, *Grand Forks, N.D.*
Mike Possin, *St. Cloud, Minn.*
Travis Roche, *Whitecourt, Alta.*
Aaron Schneekloth, *Calgary, Alta.*
Tim Skarperud, *Grand Forks, N.D.*
Kevin Spiewak, *Schaumberg, Ill.*
Jason Ulmer, *Wilcox, Sask.*
Jeff Yurecko, *Edina, Minn.*
Head coach: **Dean Blais**
Associate head coach: **Scott Sandelin**
Assistant coaches: **Jeff Bowen and Lee Davidson**
Head trainer: **Mark Poolman**
Strength coach: **Paul Chapman**
Equipment manager: **Lee Greseth**

Minneapolis, with a victory over Niagara (N.Y.) University, the upstart from the East Coast.

Wisconsin, meanwhile, suffered UND's fate of the two previous seasons, falling in its first game of the regionals despite being a seeded team.

Blais had to play a game of musical goalies late in the season, however, when both Goehring and Andy Kollar suffered concussions and other injuries.

Kollar backstopped the Sioux through the WCHA playoffs and the NCAA regional victory over Niagara. Then Goehring took over, blanking Maine in the NCAA Frozen Four semifinals and holding Boston (Mass.) College to two goals in the title game.

Just as in 1997, when senior goalie Toby Kvalevog stepped aside to let freshman Aaron Schweitzer take over the team, Kollar gracefully handed the reins to Goehring in the Frozen Four.

"That was very unselfish on his part, to step aside and say, 'Yeah, Karl's the goalie'," Blais said.

Unlike the 1997 team, this squad had size. Blais had "twin towers" on defense in 6-foot-4, 210-pound O'Connell and 6-foot-4, 225-pound Mike Commodore. They were as feared a tandem as ever has played at UND.

It was a team with snipers up front, too. Junior center Jeff Panzer led the WCHA in scoring, and senior Lee Goren led the league and the nation in goals.

Ulmer, a senior, rang up 57 points on the season, more than doubling his previous career best at UND. He teamed with Goren and freshman Ryan Bayda to form UND's most prolific line.

Blais said he thought before the season began that UND could contend for national honors. "I was really happy with the defensemen we had back, and I thought we'd have enough offense," Blais said. "Then Karl Goehring had a tremendous year in goal, too."

Goehring was brilliant in the Frozen Four shutout of Maine. The Black Bears had eight power-play chances to three for the Sioux. But Goehring's 30-save shutout was vintage Karl, the little guy from Apple Valley, Minn., making the game look easy.

Still, UND had to rally from a 2-1 deficit in the third

Amid a pile of legs, skates and sticks, little Karl Goehring, an All-America goalie in 2000, makes another save during UND's NCAA title run in Providence, R.I., that season. Goehring allowed just two goals in two games in the Frozen Four. (photo, Chuck Kimmerle, Grand Forks Herald)

Opposite: Captain may I? You most certainly can. And captain Peter Armbrust did, hugging the 2000 NCAA championship trophy. Armbrust, of Edina, Minn., played on NCAA title teams as both a freshman and a senior. (photo, Eric Hylden, Grand Forks Herald)

Lee Goren, chosen the Most Outstanding Player in the 2000 NCAA tournament won by UND, originally gave Michigan Tech a verbal commitment to play for the Huskies before changing his mind and signing with the Sioux.

period to beat Boston College and win the title. "I thought we had carried the play to them," Blais said. "I thought we deserved that game."

Goren, with two goals in the championship game, capped a season of honors by being named Most Outstanding Player in the tournament. He also was the Most Valuable Player in the WCHA Final Five and MVP of the Badger Showdown over Christmas in Milwaukee, a tournament won by the Sioux.

"He was the difference," Blais said.

Once again, UND's national success made it harder for the Sioux to follow it up the next season.

After the 2000 season, Commodore gave up his final season of eligibility to sign with the New Jersey Devils of the NHL.

"If we had had him in 2001, I think we would have won again," Blais said. "Sometimes, one player can make that big of a difference, both in play and in leadership."

But 2000 was something special.

"This title was really unexpected," Blais said. "Six weeks before we won it, we could have never dreamed of this after losing the WCHA title to Wisconsin. Instead of getting down and bummed out, it worked in reverse. The guys kicked it into gear and got it done."

None found a higher gear than Goren.

"Big players play key roles in big games," Blais said, "and Lee is a big player."

In 1997, Goren practiced with the Sioux but couldn't play the entire year because of an NCAA ruling.

So, while the Sioux celebrated the 1997 title, he was a spectator.

In 2000, he was the best player in the biggest game. Finally, he could experience the feeling of being a champion himself.

"I now know how the seniors on the 1997 team felt," Goren said. "Just to be in their shoes is an amazing experience."

UND's Jason Ulmer slides toward the net just as the puck bounces out of it in the championship game of the 2000 NCAA tournament. Ulmer scored the game-winning goal on this play against Boston (Mass.) College goalie Scott Clemmensen. *(photo, Eric Hylden, Grand Forks Herald)*

Opposite: *We did it! Sioux assistant captain Lee Goren — named Most Outstanding Player in the 2000 tournament — celebrates his empty-net goal to wrap up UND's national championship victory over Boston College. Goren, of Winnipeg, Man., led the country in goals that season with 34. (photo, Eric Hylden, Grand Forks Herald)*

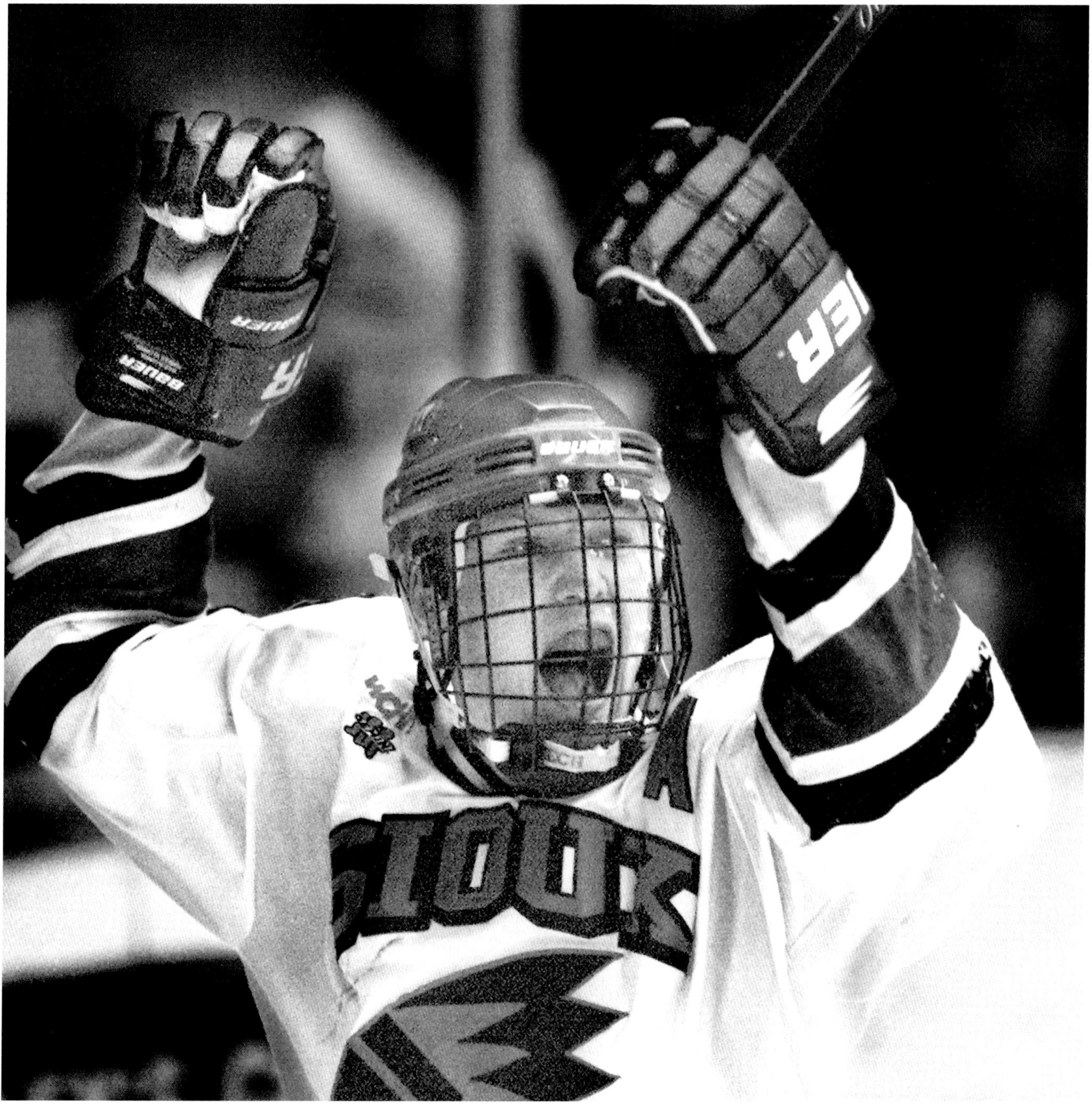
BAUER

2000 NCAA

It's party time! The Sioux begin their celebration on the bench in the closing seconds of the victory over Boston (Mass.) College in the 2000 NCAA title game. (photo, Eric Hylden, Grand Forks Herald)

Opposite: *The Sioux hockey team makes its first visit in history to the White House in 2000 on a special invitation, and coach Dean Blais presents President Bill Clinton with a Fighting Sioux jersey. Here, with Blais for the jersey presentation, is Brad DeFauw, a member of the championship team. (photo, White House)*

"If we had had him (Mike Commodore) in 2001,
I think we would have won again. Sometimes,
one player can make that big of a difference,
both in play and in leadership."

Coach Dean Blais

2000

Providence Civic Center
Providence, R.I.
April 8, 2000

North Dakota 4, Boston College 2

UND finishes second to Wisconsin in the WCHA regular-season race but wins when it counts the most. On April 8, 2000, coach Dean Blais' Sioux win their seventh NCAA title overall and third crown captured in Providence, R.I. A 4-2 victory over Boston (Mass.) College in the title game wraps it up. Lee Goren, tournament Most Outstanding Player, scores two goals.
(photo, UND Athletics)

Sioux senior wing Lee Goren said that for much of the game, he "couldn't put the puck in the ocean."

But when it mattered the most, the best player from sea to shining sea in college hockey on April 8 was the same Lee Goren.

He scored two goals in the third period as the Sioux rallied from a 2-1 deficit with three straight goals to claim their second national title in four years.

Goren's first goal at 2:43 of the third period tied the game at 2-all. He took rookie wing Ryan Bayda's drop pass and threaded a shot through the skates of Boston (Mass.) College goalie Scott Clemmensen (32 saves).

"I thought that goal energized them," Boston College coach Jerry York said.

If that goal energized the Sioux, the next two were positively electrifying.

Goren's center, Jason Ulmer, slammed in a long rebound left by

Clemmensen on Goren's initial shot at 14:22 of the period to put UND in the lead for the first time at 3-2.

Goren's empty-net goal with 46 seconds left clinched it and broke the hearts of Boston College, seeking its first NCAA title since 1949.

Goren's final goal was his 34th of the season, tops in the country.

UND had taken the first lead on a goal by 6-foot-4, 225-pound defenseman Mike Commodore at 3:48 into the game.

But the Eagles flew by the Sioux with goals by Jeff Farkas at 16:47 of the first period and Marty Hughes at 6:59 of the second for a 2-1 margin after two periods.

"We came into the locker room after the second period and said that we still had a shot," Goren said. "We said, 'Win the period, win the game,' pretty much."

Goren remembered having to sit out the 1997 season at UND but being in the stands when the Sioux scored five second-period goals to beat Boston University 6-4 in the title game in Milwaukee.

"I told the guys tonight that we can score four goals in a period," Goren said. "We scored five goals in 1997 against BU, and I knew we could do that against these guys."

They didn't need to. Three goals were plenty to give the Sioux their seventh national title.

The following day, the headline in the Grand Forks (N.D.) Herald read: "Magnificent 7th."

Goren, named the Most Outstanding Player in the tournament, capped his career with his three-point title game. He said it was a birthday present for his father, Chuck, celebrating his 50th birthday that night in the Providence stands.

Joining Goren on the all-tournament team were Commodore, forward Bryan Lundbohm and goalie Karl Goehring (21 saves).

It also was quite a sendoff for Tim O'Connell, Peter Armbrust, Brad DeFauw and Ulmer. They won NCAA titles coming and going at UND. They were freshmen on UND's 1997 title team, then exited college hockey as seniors with another crown.

It was a hard loss for Boston College to swallow, the Eagles still living with the weight of no national title since 1949.

Semifinals

		Maine (27-7-5)
	Finals	**Providence, R.I.** April 6
	North Dakota 2-0	North Dakota (29-8-5)
North Dakota 4-2	**Providence, R.I.** April 8	St. Lawrence (27-7-2)
National champion		**Providence, R.I.** April 6
	Boston College 4-2	Boston College (28-11-1)

Inside the game

Saves: North Dakota (Karl Goehring, 21); Boston College (Scott Clemmensen, 32).
Total penalties: North Dakota 7 for 14 minutes; Boston College 4 for 8 minutes.
Power plays: North Dakota 0 for 3; Boston College 1 for 6.
Officials: Matt Shegos (referee), Bill Jones (assistant referee), Jeff Fulton (assistant referee).
Attendance: 11,484.

1st

Goals
1. ND, Mike Commodore (Bryan Lundbolm, Tim Skarperud) 3:48; 2. BC, Jeff Farkas (Blake Bellefeuille, Brian Gionta) 16:47 (pp).

Penalties
ND, Aaron Schneekloth (cross checking) 6:32; BC, Jeff Giuliano (hooking) 10:02; ND, Ryan Bayda (slashing) 11:35; ND, Chad Mazurak (high sticking) 16:28; BC, Jeff Giuliano (hooking) 17:13.

2nd

Goals
3. BC, Marty Hughes (Gionta) 6:59.

Penalties
ND, Mazurak (holding) :25; ND, Tim O'Connell (slashing) 3:04; BC, Bench (too many men, served by Hughes) 4:21; BC, Ales Dolinar (slashing) 10:45; ND, Commodore (holding) 10:45; ND, Commodore (tripping) 14:26.

3rd

Goals
4. ND, Lee Goren (Bayda) 2:43; 5. ND, Jason Ulmer (Goren) 14:22; 6. ND, Goren (unassisted) 19:14 (en).

The new Ralph Engelstad Arena becomes the second rink to bear the former UND goalie's name. The Winter Sports Center, which opened in 1972, was renamed Ralph Engelstad Arena in 1988 after Engelstad pledged more than $5 million to the UND hockey program.

Through the eyes of a goaltender, this is how the action looks in old Engelstad Arena. Sioux goalie Karl Goehring makes a save against Minnesota on a shot captured from a camera mounted inside the net. (photo, Scott Fredrickson)

Lord of the rinks *1936-2001*

Befitting a college with a tradition of great hockey, UND will reach the "hat trick" in indoor rinks in its lifetime, with the opening of the new Ralph Engelstad Arena in the fall of 2001.

The new Engelstad Arena is unquestionably the most elaborate, most costly, biggest and best of them all.

But that doesn't mean there aren't rich memories associated with UND's two earlier rinks.

Both can stake claim as being "the best" of their times, in one form or another.

The Winter Sports Building was affectionately known by many as the "barn," or sometimes, "the igloo."

"For a place with no cows, UND did have a barn," reads one article in the archives of UND's University Relations department.

Built in 1936 as a Works Projects Administration job at a cost of $43,000, it was used from 1936 until 1972. The final game found UND beating the University of Michigan 10-2 in the WCHA playoffs — Grand Forks' Gary Purpur scoring the last goal ever there.

The bitter cold inside the building was legendary. "Inside what the North Dakota fans call 'The Igloo,' " wrote Jim Tandall in the Michigan student newspaper in 1966, "it is impossible to tell whether the spectators and combatants are really blue, or whether it is just the mercury vapor lights that give that impression."

Al Purpur, who tended the ice there for 39 years, once explained that the cold may have been overemphasized. "I think it was the dampness more than the cold," Purpur said. "When I put down a new sheet of water, the dampness would hang in the air. That's what made people think it was colder than it was."

The building seated only 4,000, so fans huddled to stay warm. Smoking was permitted inside, lending to the blue haze mentioned by the student newspaper writer.

This rink was home to UND's first two NCAA championship

teams in 1959 and 1963. UND played 394 games in the Winter Sports Building, winning 254, losing 118 and tying 22 there, for a .673 winning percentage.

Visiting teams weren't used to playing in unheated indoor rinks and in front of such exuberant fans as those jammed into the UND rink. "Thus, North Dakota will continue to have a tremendous home-ice advantage, having loyal fans and being used to the cold," Michigan's Tandall wrote.

The "barn" served as a storage building for six years after UND's second indoor rink opened in the fall of 1972. That rink was called the Winter Sports Center until it was renamed Ralph Engelstad Arena in 1988.

When the "barn" was torn down in 1978, it cost nearly $30,000 to demolish, not much less than the money spent to construct it.

In a survey of Western Collegiate Hockey Association teams conducted by the league in 1999, seven of 10 captains named the old Engelstad Arena as either their favorite arena to play in or the toughest setting for a visiting team.

That's high praise indeed and a tribute to the design of the old rink, where every seat was a good one.

With the advent of the new Engelstad Arena and the phasing out of the old one, the question remains to be answered as to whether the intimate, fan-friendly atmosphere in old Engelstad Arena will carry over.

The 6,067-seat Engelstad Arena was home to the Fighting Sioux from 1972 through the 2000-2001 season. It was home to NCAA championship teams in 1980, 1982, 1987, 1997 and 2000, so it saw its share of celebrations, along with occasional heartbreaks.

All told, there were 593 official games played in Engelstad Arena — most of them won by the Sioux. In the 29 seasons the rink was home to the Sioux, UND carved out exactly 400 victories against 171 losses and 22 ties there, for a winning percentage of .693.

The Sioux opened the rink on Nov. 10, 1972. Roseau's (Minn.) Earl Anderson, a tri-captain of coach Rube Bjorkman's team, scored the first Sioux goal in a 5-4 win over Colorado College. The final official game played there came in the 2000-2001 season, a 4-0 victory over the University of Minnesota-Duluth to wrap up the best-of-three WCHA playoff series in UND's favor.

In the old Winter Sports Building, fashion gives way to the practicality of remaining warm. (photo, UND Special Collections)

Grand Forks' own Jeff Panzer, a Hobey Baker finalist and two-time All-America selection at center, scored the last goal in the rink on an unassisted breakaway in a game on March 11, 2001. Senior record-setting goalie Karl Goehring made 25 saves for his 14th career shutout.

The rink had a glorious tradition. It not only was home to the

This photograph from 1966 offers a panoramic view of the interior of the Winter Sports Building, UND's first indoor rink. From the looks of it, it's another sellout crowd. (photo, UND Athletics)

Sioux, but to the North Dakota state high school hockey tournament. It also was the site of the 1983 NCAA Division I hockey tournament, the only time UND has held the event.

The arena's construction cost $1.9 million — $1.1 million of it provided by private donations and the balance pledged through student bonds. By pledging nearly half the cost of the rink, UND students were given nearly half of the seats in the building, certainly adding to the hostile setting for visiting teams.

The late John O'Keefe, the father of current Sioux hockey color commentator Tim O'Keefe, was chairman of the drive to raise the $1.1 million in private funds. Those who donated $100 or more had their names inscribed on hockey pucks that were mounted on the walls inside the rink.

In 1983, a foyer was added to the front of the rink at a cost of $750,000. That money came from the UND Foundation.

Called the Winter Sports Center for 16 years after opening in 1972, it was renamed the Ralph Engelstad Arena by action of the North Dakota Board of Higher Education in 1988. That action came after a

pledge in excess of $5 million from Engelstad, a former UND goalie from Thief River Falls, Minn., for use by the hockey program.

Initial cost estimates for the new Ralph Engelstad Arena were $60 million. To date, the price tag is closer to $100 million — and the builder-owner might not really care.

He set out to build the finest college rink in the nation, and he has with The House That Ralph Built.

It's part of a gift pledged to UND by Ralph and Betty Engelstad of Las Vegas, Nev.

The building was designed by Schoen Associates of Grand Forks, N.D., and built by Ralph Engelstad Arena Inc. — Engelstad's company put together to construct and run the rink until he turns it over to UND.

Among the features:

Five stories and 400,000 square feet;

Seating for 11,400;

Forty-eight luxury boxes;

Four additional rental suites;

Adjacent Olympic-size (200-by-100-foot) practice and rental rink next to the main rink;

A pro shop, and Sioux tradition-Hall of Fame display;

A state-of-the-art locker room for the Sioux, featuring nearly every piece of exercise equipment on the market. In addition, a hot tub and sauna inside the locker room — each big enough to hold the entire team;

Eight auxiliary locker rooms, plus the Sioux room and the locker room for the visitors;

A $1 million, eight-sided, show-stealing scoreboard hanging over the center of the rink, showing replays and other highlights;

A seamless, full-color LED video ring displaying league scores, statistics and other information encircling the lower bowl;

Four escalators and four elevators carrying fans from the main concourse to the upper level, which will hold 4,600 fans compared with 5,800 for the lower level;

Eighteen restrooms, 10 on the main level, eight on the upper level;

Sixteen concession stands, eight on each level;

Cast iron, upholstered armchairs with cupholders.

There are bigger rinks than this one — but, most likely, none better.

UND cheerleaders Jeannie Anderson (left) and Sandy Roller, both from Grand Forks, N.D., sport a Camelot look with their Jackie Kennedy-style hats as they watch the Sioux in the late 1960s during the final years in the Winter Sports Building. (photo, UND Special Collections)

Sioux hockey fans don't mind standing outside in the cold to buy tickets for a UND game in 1953. They aren't camera shy, either. (photo, UND Special Collections)

Opposite: *A digital rendering shows the new state-of-the-art Engelstad Arena in Grand Forks, N.D. (photo, Bob Caulfield; digital retouching, Jerry Olson)*

It took two referees to control UND's Dean Dachyshyn when the Sioux hard-hitting wing wanted to do more than play the game. Here, referees Dewey Markus (left) and Dick Haig put their efforts into getting Dachyshyn under control against Wisconsin's Tim Thomas. Dachyshyn ranks among the top five in career leaders at UND in penalties. (photo, bill alkofer, Dakota Student)

Shortly after Dean Dachyshyn got into a brawl in the penalty box at UND, coach John "Gino" Gasparini had a partition built, separating the two sides of the box. It became known as the "Dachyshyn wall."

Tough guys, tough talk

How close to the edge was the University of North Dakota's Jim Archibald when he was on his way to becoming the most penalized player in NCAA hockey history?

Well, let's take a look at an off-ice story involving the man known as "Archie."

While hunting near his home in Canada, Archibald wounded a deer with his final shell. The deer kept running.

And Archibald? He ran, too. He chased down the deer on foot, jumped on its back and cut its throat with his knife.

"That story is absolutely true," said UND coach Dean Blais, who has hunted with Archibald.

That tells you the mind-set with which Archibald managed to run up 247 penalties and 540 total minutes — still school records — in his 1981-1985 career at UND.

At a school where tough guys such as Mike Commodore, Craig Ludwig, Dean Dachyshyn, Dan Brennan and Howard Walker all played with a high degree of intimidation, nobody teetered more on the edge than Archibald.

"(Archibald) is the one who comes to mind (when recalling players who were on the edge)," said Blais, an assistant UND coach when Archibald wore the Sioux jersey, "not only because of his penalty minutes, but because he was feared by other teams."

At 5 foot 11, 185 pounds, Archibald was a giant in terms of killer instinct. He was a key contributor in other areas, too. He finished with 75 goals and 69 assists for 144 points in 154 career games, leading the Sioux in goals, points — and, of course, penalties — in his senior season. Opponents, Blais said, gave Archibald room to maneuver, based on his reputation for the rough stuff.

But Blais remembers another side of Archibald. He said he was an intelligent young man, articulate, and one of the few players he remembers who never missed a single class at UND (when the Sioux weren't on

the road). The Craik, Sask., native went on to play in the National Hockey League with the Minnesota North Stars.

Blais said opponents feared Archibald because of his tenacity — and toughness. "Archie would rather hit you and hurt you than score a goal," Blais said.

Archibald would look for someone to hit — anywhere on the ice — Blais said. "Archie would come off his right wing, over to the left wing side, just to hit you. And he'd always try to hit the best players on the other team, regardless of how big they were."

East Grand Forks, Minn., native Jeff Bowen was a teammate of Archibald's during the 1984-1985 season. In Orono, Maine, he witnessed a bench-emptying brawl between the Sioux and the Black Bears of Maine. Archibald and Scott Sandelin were serving as Sioux captains.

That brawl came right after Christmas. So much for being the season to be jolly. The Sioux were in a fighting mood.

"Archie was beating up on two or three guys," Bowen said. "I remember grabbing him, and yelling 'Archie! Archie!'," Bowen said.

Bowen got no response. "I looked in his eyes, and there was nobody home," Bowen said. "That happened more than once. He was a little psycho."

That same season, UND opened the year at Providence (R.I.) College.

Following warm-ups for the two teams, Archibald was leaning on the boards, waiting for the rest of the players to leave the ice first.

A Providence College arena worker who came onto the ice to brush and scrape along the boards made the mistake of pushing his broom into Archibald's skates.

"Archie popped him right in the nose, knocking him down," said Tarek Howard, a defenseman on that team. "Archie hit him pretty good. I think the guy was looking for something. He certainly didn't expect what he got."

Though referees and coaches weren't present near the ice, Archibald still was given a 10-minute misconduct penalty to start the game. The penalty was handed out based on accounts from eyewitnesses and from the ice attendant.

"You never knew what Archie would do," Howard said. "Some guys are tough because of their size. Archie wasn't big. He was just very tough."

Because Blais had recruited Archibald, head coach John "Gino" Gasparini often sent Blais to try to calm him down.

"It was like walking into a lion's den," Blais said. "You never knew if he'd fly off the handle — even at a coach — though he never did."

Archibald might be the most famous villain to play college hockey or, certainly, the most infamous at UND.

But other guys had their mean streaks.

David Christian, one of the stars of the 1978-1979 UND team that won a Western Collegiate Hockey Association championship, looks at the action on the ice. (photo, Ron Smith, Grand Forks Herald)

I can't breathe! UND's Jim Archibald seems to have a chokehold on Badger Vic Posa as Wisconsin coach Jeff Sauer moves in from the right to lend assistance during this game in the mid-1980s in Grand Forks, N.D. (photo, bill alkofer, Dakota Student)

When Dean Dachyshyn took one of his many penalties during his 1979-1983 career that included two NCAA championship rings, he got into a brawl with a University of Wisconsin player in the penalty box at UND.

Shortly after that, Gasparini had a partition built, separating the two sides of the penalty box. It became known as the "Dachyshyn wall."

Times have changed. Back in the days of Archibald, Dachyshyn and Walker, a good fight was penalized by a double or triple minor penalty. Now, a game disqualification goes with a fight. That's made would-be fighters more fearful of dropping the gloves.

Commodore, at 6 foot 4, 225 pounds, commanded respect on the ice, and players feared him.

When Wisconsin's Alex Brooks challenged Commodore on the ice at UND, the challenge was answered quickly. With one punch, Commodore shattered Brooks' nose.

Some players combined toughness with tough talk, which could be just as effective.

In 1979, UND and the University of Minnesota were playing in the final game of the WCHA season in Minneapolis, with the league title on the line. Walker, the fierce-looking Sioux defenseman with a Fu Manchu, talked the talk just as Gopher rookie center Neal Broten was about to take

Jim Archibald, who played at UND from 1981 to 1985, finished his career as the most penalized player in NCAA history with 247 penalties for a total of 540 minutes. Of his 247 career penalties, 159 of them came in his final two seasons.

Opposite: Former Sioux goalie Ed Belfour hoists the Stanley Cup high after his Dallas Stars win the NHL playoff championship in 1999, beating Buffalo in the finals. Belfour, Tony Hrkac and Craig Ludwig — all three of them former Sioux — played together with Dallas in 1999. A fourth former Sioux player, Rick Wilson, was an assistant coach with Dallas. (photo, Tom Pennington, Fort Worth Star-Telegram)

a key draw. "Broten," Walker growled, "if you go into the corner after the puck, it'll be the last thing you do in your life."

In an NCAA regional playoff game against Colorado College, Sioux 5-foot-9, 175-pound wing Jason Notermann was assigned as a checker against Colorado's top line, which included bruising 6-foot-3, 210-pound Justin Morrison.

Notermann hit Morrison so hard that he knocked him out of action for the remainder of one period.

When Colorado coach Scott Owens put Chris Hartsburg out on the line to replace Morrison, Notermann didn't waste time, or words.

"You got a lot of balls," Notermann told Hartsburg. "Didn't you see what happened to the last winger they sent out against me?"

Neither Hartsburg nor Morrison picked up a single point against Notermann in a 4-1 victory that sent the Sioux on to the Frozen Four.

Many other tough guys have worn the Sioux jersey. Former Minnesota Gopher coach Herb Brooks calls Bill Steenson the toughest defenseman he's ever played against, for example. Brooks played for Minnesota when Steenson played for UND in the late 1950s.

Yes, UND had tough guys — and some tough games.

Take the "water bottle game" that took place between the Sioux and the University of Wisconsin on Jan. 30, 1982, in Dane County Coliseum in Madison, Wis.

In a year in which two of the most talented teams in college history (the 1982 Sioux and Wisconsin Badgers) later clashed in the NCAA title game, the real battle was earlier in Madison.

It began when Wisconsin's John Newberry squirted water from a bottle on the bench into the face of UND tough guy and team captain Cary Eades — twice.

The second time, Eades simply flew into the Wisconsin bench when the door opened for a line change and challenged the entire team to a fight. Earlier, Newberry and Eades — who had played junior hockey against each other in British Columbia — had exchanged verbal blows.

"I just remember the bench door was wide open and, unfortunately, that gave me a natural pathway to ask John if what I heard him say to me was accurate," Eades later told Madison sportswriter Bill Brophy.

"The next thing I knew, Eades is on the bench — and holy smokes," Newberry said.

"It wasn't my brightest move ever," Eades says today.

A series of battles raged on the ice for a long time, featuring such heavyweights as UND's Eades, Ludwig, Brennan and Archibald against the likes of Newberry and Pat Ethier.

No divider separated the two benches, so the battle spilled over easily from one bench to the other.

At one point, three Madison police officers dragged Archibald off the ice and down under the stands, by the beer garden, where Archibald got into it with the fans. Just when it appeared as though calm was

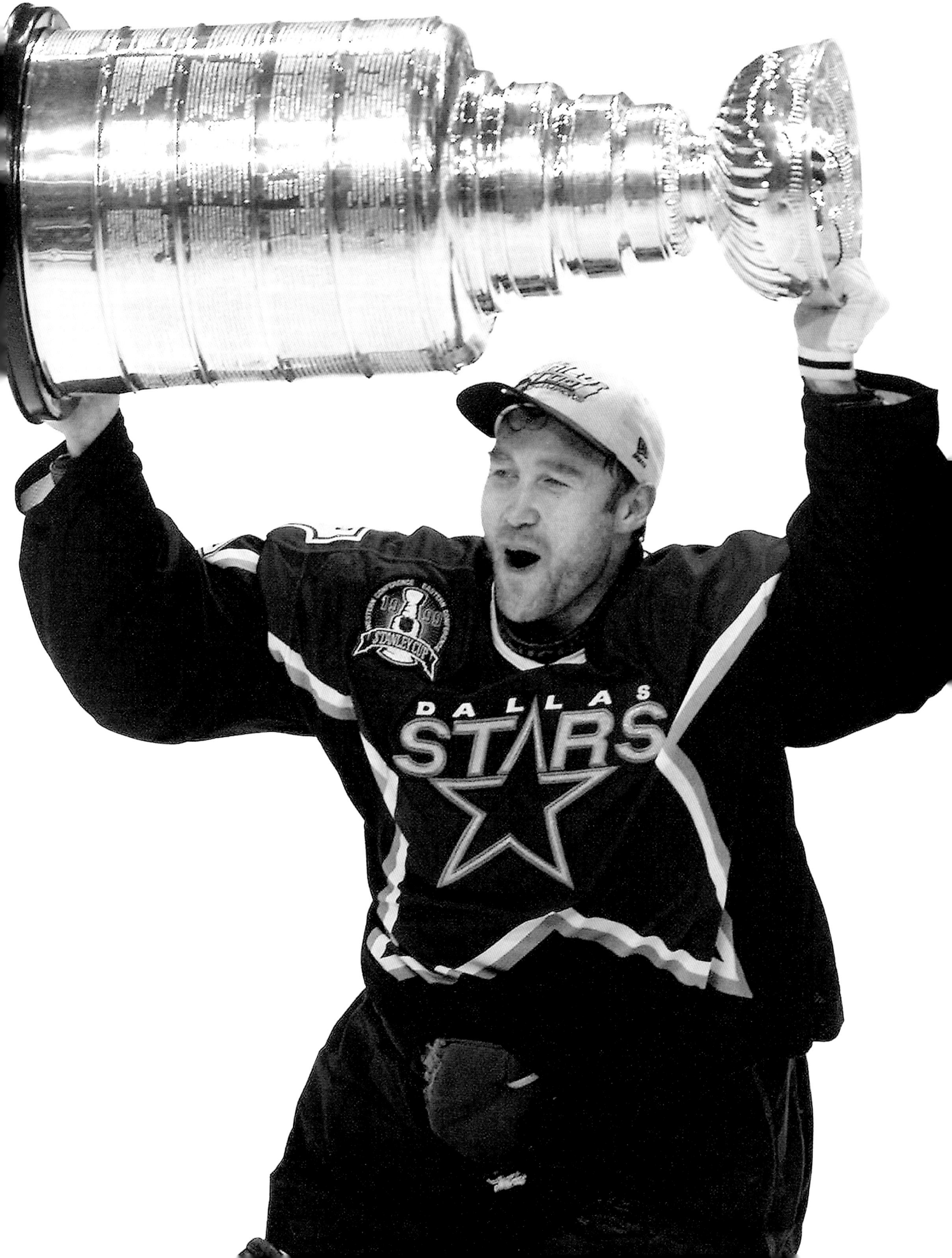
DALLAS
STARS

Two of UND's tough guys — Jim Archibald (15) and Dan Brennan (right) — watch from the bench as the action proceeds on the ice in Engelstad Arena. Sandwiched between Archibald and Brennan is Dunstan "Dusty" Carroll, the only Sioux player ever from Prince Edward Island. (photo, bill alkofer, Dakota Student)

"They were two great teams and a lot of great players, but everyone still talks about the water bottle (incident). It was kind of like all-star wrestling."

Cary Eades, 1978-1982

restored, the infamous Archibald reignited the sparks.

Blais and John Marks, UND assistant coaches that year, were sitting up in the stands when the brawl began. They quickly made their way to ice level.

"The first thing I saw," Blais said, "was Archibald running back across the concrete by the beer garden and back onto the ice. He sucker-punched a guy right by the bench, and it all started up again."

All told, Brennan, Eades and Archibald from UND and Newberry, Ethier and Steve McKenzie of Wisconsin were given game disqualifications by referees Medo Martinello and Larry Paradise.

Later, WCHA chief referee Dewey Markus tacked on an additional five-game suspension for Archibald and two-game suspensions for Newberry and Eades.

Even in the broadcast booth high in the stands, the tension was thick.

Sportscaster Ed Schultz of Fargo, N.D., televising the game back to North Dakota, got carried away with his accounts of the brawl. Unfortunately, his press seat was in the middle of the stands, so the Wisconsin fans surrounding him soon turned on him verbally.

One fan, in particular, irritated Schultz. "I'd like to bop that bozo!" Schultz said, in one of his more famous lines.

Even after order was restored, Wisconsin's Todd Lecy used his stick to shoot the Sioux gloves that were strewn on the ice into the stands.

Finally, the public-address announcer asked fans to return the gear, or the game wouldn't resume. From high in the stands, the gloves came flying back down, one by one.

"They were two great teams and a lot of great players," Eades said. "But everyone still talks about the water bottle (incident). It was kind of like all-star wrestling."

Almost lost in that game, won 3-0 by Wisconsin, was one of the strangest goals against the Sioux in history.

With seconds left in the second period and Wisconsin leading 2-0, the Sioux were on the power play. In the Wisconsin defensive zone, Badger Ken Keryluk won a faceoff and drew the puck back to defenseman Chris Chelios, who was one stride inside the Badger goal line.

Chelios cranked a high slap shot from 190 feet away that sailed the length of the ice, bounced once, changed directions and skipped by Sioux goalie Jon Casey for a shorthanded goal of epic proportions.

Wisconsin fans cranked up their "sieve, sieve, sieve!" chant. Poor Casey.

"I remember (Sioux center) Troy Murray coming back to the bench and saying, 'Sorry I lost the faceoff,' " Eades recalled. "We all kind of laughed."

But the brawl itself was no laughing matter. "It was a good thing that Dean Dachyshyn (a Sioux tough guy who was out with an injury) wasn't with us on that trip — or the fight might still be going on," Eades says today.

Great stories never wear out and are retold for years to come.

Oh, he's big! That seems to be the reaction of two Boston (Mass.) College players, as they take a look at the menacing frame of 6-foot-4, 225-pound Mike Commodore during a Sioux practice at the 2000 NCAA Frozen Four in Providence, R.I. With Commodore is Bryan Lundbohm, who later was named to the all-tournament team along with Commodore. (photo, Eric Hylden, Grand Forks Herald)

When the Hockey
Hall of Fame in
Canada asked former
Sioux defenseman
Craig Ludwig for the
UND-issued shin
guards he wore in
more than 1,200
NHL games, he
refused to hand
them over.

Friendships form, bonds are built, memories are made.

So, it was like a trip down memory lane in 1999, when the Dallas Stars met the Buffalo Sabres in the Stanley Cup Finals.

No fewer than six former Sioux players were on the rosters of the two teams who met in Marine Midland Arena in Buffalo, N.Y., and at Reunion Arena in Dallas, Texas, before the Stars prevailed.

Assistant coach Rick Wilson, goalie Ed Belfour, defenseman Craig Ludwig and center Tony Hrkac played for Dallas, while former Sioux James Patrick and Dixon Ward were skating for Buffalo.

They were too busy battling each other for pro hockey's most storied trophy to reminisce much about their days at UND, but their warm feelings surfaced when they had a few moments.

Ward described his UND days this way: "I learned the game from Gino Gasparini. I didn't know the game when I went there. He gave me a good work ethic, a good foundation to learn it even more. There's no question that Gino taught me what the game was all about. He taught me how to be successful."

Tony Hrkac, the only UND player to win the Hobey Baker Memorial Award as the nation's best player, still carries fond memories of Grand Forks, N.D., and UND.

People in Grand Forks still ask about Hrkac. They do elsewhere in the country, too. Anyone who has followed college hockey for a long time won't forget the Hrkac Circus, UND's 1987 national championship team led by Hrkac.

In fact, Hrkac ranks as one of the most popular players ever to play at UND.

He credits his popularity in part to his friendship with Grand Forks native Steve Johnson, a teammate at UND. "Since Steve was from Grand Forks, I got to meet a lot of people in town away from school and hockey," Hrkac told the Grand Forks Herald in Dallas during the 1999 Stanley Cup Finals. "Steve was pretty popular in high school, so I got to meet all his friends and his friends' friends. I think that was the biggest reason."

Ludwig took a "friend" from UND with him to the NHL.

Throughout his NHL career that spanned 17 seasons and lasted until he was 38, Ludwig wore the same pair of shin guards issued to him in 1979 by UND equipment manager Dave Kamrowski. Ludwig glued them

Defenseman Howard Walker could stop you cold with his body checks or cut off your progress with his stick. Walker uses his stick here to slow a Colorado College player. Sioux forward Erwin Martens looks on. Walker, a member of UND's 1980 NCAA championship team, signed a professional contract after his sophomore season. (photo, John Stennes, Grand Forks Herald)

hundreds of times, patching cracks.

But he kept wearing them. For more than 1,200 NHL games, they protected the shot-blocking defenseman against the game's hardest shooters.

"I can't even read the brand name on them anymore," Ludwig said. "All I know is that they still work."

He obviously became attached to those shin guards. When the Hockey Hall of Fame in Canada asked Ludwig to send them for inclusion in its display, he refused.

Belfour, too, remembers his UND days fondly.

And after Dallas won the NHL title that season, Belfour brought the Stanley Cup to Grand Forks — and to UND — to share it with the fans and the program that gave him his start toward greatness.

That tells you two things: Many of these players were special at UND. And UND is special to them.

Just a win away *1958-2001*

The 2000-2001 season featured a historic trip to the White House by Sioux coaches and team captains Karl Goehring and Jeff Panzer to meet President Clinton. They were joined by six players now playing professional hockey who were part of the 2000 title team.

Opposite: Even in good times, there are sad times. Senior captain Jeff Panzer of Grand Forks, N.D., was a Hobey Baker Memorial Award finalist in the 2000-2001 season, an All-America selection and the Western Collegiate Hockey Association's Player of the Year. But those honors don't stop the tears from flowing after the Sioux lose 3-2 in overtime to Boston (Mass.) College in the 2001 NCAA championship game in Albany, N.Y. It was the final game in a Sioux uniform for Panzer, who finished his career as one of the school's all-time great players. (photo, John Stennes, Grand Forks Herald)

T he excitement generated by a team winning a national championship is one thing. It's quite another for a team to enjoy the ride all the way to the final and then fall just short.

The Sioux have done that four times since the 1957-1958 season.

It happened in 1978-1979, when first-year head coach John "Gino" Gasparini and his UND Fighting Sioux lost to the University of Minnesota 4-3 in the NCAA championship game in Detroit, Mich.

While the title eluded those Sioux, the thrill of the ride did not.

For Gasparini, the rookie head coach after being Rube Bjorkman's longtime assistant, the pain of losing in the finals wasn't so hurtful.

"We'd never experienced winning to the extent we did that year for a long time," Gasparini said. "It was a fun thing to watch."

UND could have clinched the WCHA title outright that season at home but lost 6-5 to Michigan State. "I remember that for being Amo Bessone's last trip to Grand Forks as (Spartan) coach," Gasparini said.

"Carl Miller (UND athletic director) wanted to make a big presentation to Amo between the second and third periods of that game," Gasparini said. "I begged him to do it at Sioux Boosters or someplace else. But they honored Amo between the second and third periods of the Saturday game, and they came out and just smoked us in the third period."

That loss on the books, UND needed to win one of two games at Minnesota the following weekend to win its first WCHA title since 1967. The Gophers beat UND 5-2 the first night, but the Sioux won the rematch 4-2 to clinch the title. David Christian's empty-net slap shot in the closing seconds secured the title.

But exactly three weeks later, UND lost to those same Gophers 4-3 in Detroit to fall short of a national crown — a goal by Roseau, Minn., native Neal Broten turning out to be the winner.

In 1957-1958, the Sioux lost 6-2 to fellow WCHA member Denver (Colo.) University in the title game in Minneapolis after beating the

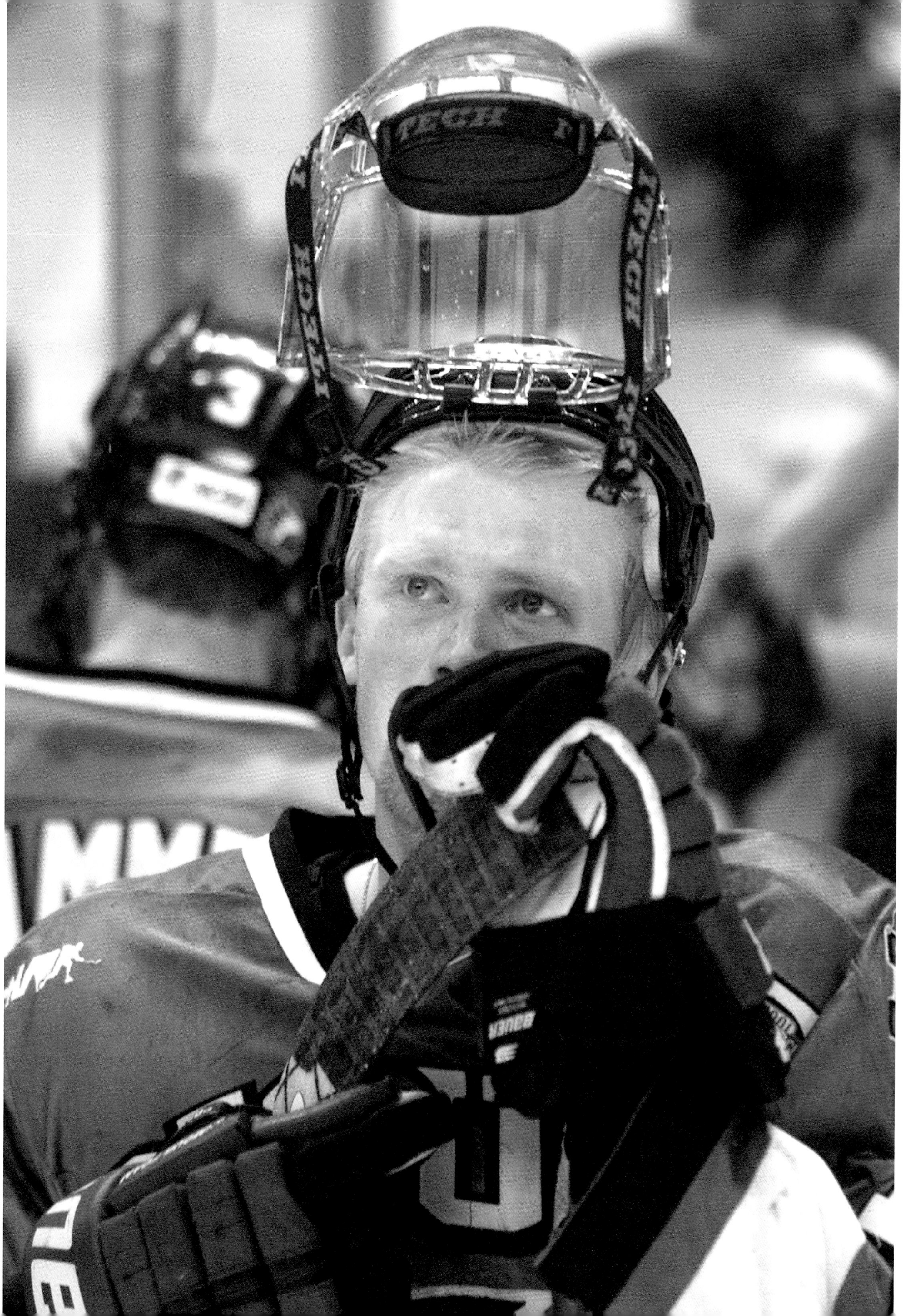
TECH
BAUER

It took an overtime goal by Boston (Mass.) College sophomore Krys Kolonas in the 2001 Frozen Four final to give the Eagles a 3-2 win over the Sioux and prevent UND from becoming the first college team since Boston (Mass.) University in 1971 and 1972 to win back-to-back titles.

Pioneers three out of four meetings during the regular season — once by 9-0.

In 1959, UND won its first NCAA title in Troy, N.Y.

But the failure of the 1958 team to win it still bothers Bob May, the Sioux coach at the time.

"We had a better team in 1958 than we did in 1959," May said. "But we weren't as strong in goal as we should have been in 1958."

In 1967-1968, Murray Armstrong's Denver Pioneers won the WCHA title with a 15-3 record, allowing just 32 goals in 18 games. UND (13-8-1) finished third, behind Michigan Tech (15-5), so the Sioux never expected to reach the NCAA Frozen Four in Duluth, Minn.

The Sioux, under coach Bill Selman, beat Cornell University 3-1 in the semifinals of the four-team NCAA tournament for the right to meet Denver again.

The Pioneers whipped Boston (Mass.) College 4-1 in the other semifinal, then blanked the Sioux 4-0 in the title game behind a 22-save performance by goalie Gerry Powers and a staunch defense led by future NHL star Keith Magnuson.

Denver scored all four of its goals in the third period against Sioux goalie Mike Curran (24 saves), the last two coming 19 seconds apart in the final two minutes.

"It was almost a duplicate of the year before when we lost to Cornell and goalie Ken Dryden 1-0 in the national semifinals," said Gasparini, a tri-captain on the 1968 team. "First goal wins."

Gasparini, who was named UND's head coach 10 years later, said Denver was outstanding on defense. "We were no slouches, either, with guys like John Marks and Terry Abram on defense," Gasparini said. "Offensively, we had some great chances, but we just couldn't get one by their goalie."

The 2000-2001 season featured a historic trip to the White House by Sioux coaches and team captains Karl Goehring and Jeff Panzer to meet with President Bill Clinton in December. They were joined by six players in pro hockey who were part of the 2000 championship team.

A season that featured a first — a trip by a Sioux hockey team to the White House — nearly ended with another first for the Sioux.

No team had repeated as NCAA champion since Boston University in 1971 and 1972, so it was a tall order for the Sioux when they won the WCHA and advanced through the league and NCAA regional playoffs to the NCAA Frozen Four in Albany, N.Y.

They drew a team on a mission in the finals in Boston College. The Eagles, who hadn't won an NCAA title since 1949, wanted this one badly, with so many fans from nearby Boston on hand.

The Eagles got it, too, downing the Sioux 3-2 in overtime on a great effort by Krys Kolanos for the winning goal at 4:43 of OT.

But fans long will remember the Sioux and coach Dean Blais for nearly pulling off the impossible.

Sioux reserve goalie Andy Kollar (right) consoles senior goalie Karl Goehring after Boston (Mass.) College's overtime goal in the 2001 NCAA championship game. The game concluded the college career for Goehring, who later signed a professional contract with the National Hockey League's Columbus Blue Jackets. (photo, John Stennes, Grand Forks Herald)

With the Sioux down 2-0 late in the third period and UND working on a power play, Blais lifted goalie Karl Goehring for a sixth attacker in a daring move.

It paid off on Grand Forks (N.D.) Red River graduate Tim Skarperud's goal at 16:18, chopping Boston College's lead to 2-1.

In the final minute of play, Blais pulled Goehring again for a sixth attacker (Wes Dorey) in a final effort to tie it. Dorey banged in a rebound from the side of the net at 19:23 of the third period, forcing overtime.

But in the extra period, Kolanos and linemate Chuck Kobasew worked a crossing pattern to perfection for the winning goal.

Of UND's four trips to the NCAA title game that came up short, this was the second time the Sioux lost by a single goal — and the first time it happened in overtime.

"There have been times I have cried after a loss," Blais said. "But this one, I can't help but think what a character-type team and year we've had."

Said captain Jeff Panzer: "It's a bad feeling, losing. But you can't look down at it, because we've accomplished more than we thought we could — or anybody thought we could."

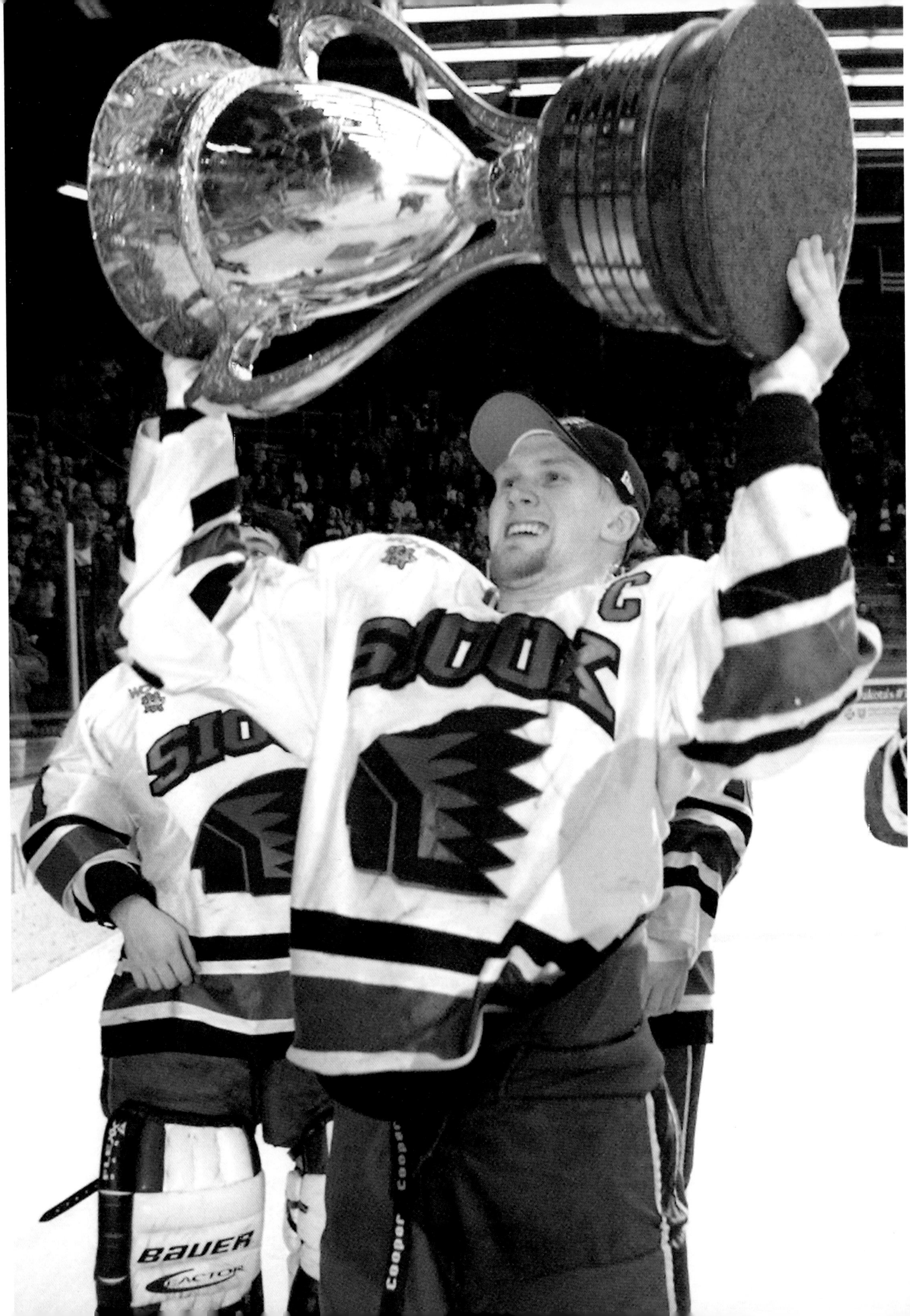
BAUER
Cooper

Home-grown talent *1930-2001*

T he Grand Forks area has been far more than just the proud home of the UND Fighting Sioux hockey team over the years.

Grand Forks, N.D., and East Grand Forks, Minn., have combined to provide 49 players who earned Fighting Sioux letters, one man who became a head coach at UND, an Olympic silver medalist and two All-Americans.

In addition, three players from Grand Forks have led the Fighting Sioux in scoring since 1946. Two of them — Steve Johnson and Jeff Panzer — led the country in scoring.

The first season of hockey at UND in which scoring records are listed was 1946-1947, when Grand Forks' Bob Grina led the Sioux in goals (13) and points (21) in 13 games.

From the early days of the legendary Cliff "Fido" Purpur to the legendary feats of his relative, Jeff Panzer, four decades later, local contributions have been rich indeed.

But none is richer than that of Fido Purpur, the only North Dakota native who has played in the National Hockey League. As a coach at UND from 1949 to 1956, he walked door to door, asking downtown merchants to support his program.

It was a dirt-poor existence for Sioux hockey at that time. Half a decade later, one of Purpur's players is turning UND's facilities into the gem of the nation. Ralph Engelstad, a goalie on Purpur's teams from 1948 to 1950, is building and donating the new Engelstad Arena to UND.

Johnson and Panzer both were finalists for the Hobey Baker Memorial Award given to the nation's top collegiate player. Johnson was a finalist in 1988, when he led the nation in scoring. Panzer was a two-time finalist — in 2000 and 2001.

Ken Purpur was never an All-America winner at UND, where he played under his older brother, Fido, from 1951 to 1954. But he certainly carved his place in history.

In 1956, the Grand Forks native was part of the U.S. hockey team

that won a silver medal in the Winter Olympics in Italy. Ken Purpur is the only Grand Forks area player who lettered in hockey at UND and won an Olympic medal in the sport.

Far more Grand Forks and East Grand Forks players own championship rings for their contributions to Sioux hockey.

Grand Forks area players who won letters on NCAA championship teams at UND are Bob Peabody and Stan Paschke (1959); Rick Myers (1980); Dean Barsness and Steve Palmiscno (1982); Jeff Bowen, Steve Johnson and Mike LaMoine (1987); Jay Panzer (1997); Jason Endres, Jeff Panzer and Tim Skarperud (2000); and Tim O'Connell (both 1997 and 2000).

East Grand Forks Senior High's Bowen has the distinction of playing on a national championship team at UND (1987) and serving as an assistant coach on another Sioux title team (2000).

Manvel, N.D., native Paul Murphy belongs on the list, too. Murphy played his high school hockey in Grand Forks and was a member of the 2000 NCAA championship team.

All told, nearly one-tenth of the players who have lettered in hockey at UND have been from either Grand Forks or East Grand Forks.

In nearly every phase of the game, you'll find big contributions made by the locals behind the scenes.

Zamboni driver Dennis Gunderson has a national reputation of excellence as a maker of ice. Long before he came on board, Al "Keys" Purpur was the ice maestro and man of many hats at UND.

Locals Wendy Feist, John Smith and Greg Powers got to know every ruffian in the Western Collegiate Hockey Association as keepers of the penalty box. Dave Kamrowski, the longtime manager in charge of player equipment, saw his share of championship hockey in his time — all the while doing his best to keep the Sioux skates sharp and the uniforms sharp-looking.

Longtime rink maintenance helper Jeff Anderson is known by thousands of former Sioux players and fans. He's a part of the hockey lore, his ready smile and uncanny memory of past players making him a walking history book and a man beloved by all.

Vi Purpur, Al's wife, worked for years as the person in charge of concessions, feeding the fans while her husband was making ice. Before that, Gene Lovejoy and his wife, Mayme, were key figures in running the fabled "barn," as the Winter Sports Building was known. Mabel Fee worked alongside Vi Purpur for years and took over her role when she retired.

From the present behind-the-scenes staff headed by Sioux hockey secretary Theresa Carter to trainer Mark Poolman to manager Mike

Grand Forks' Steve Johnson, who led the nation in scoring as a senior at UND in the 1987-1988 season, signs autographs. Johnson was a key member of UND's 1987 NCAA championship team. Today, he's a successful coach in the United States Hockey League. A number of his players from the Lincoln (Neb.) Stars team have come to UND to play for Johnson's alma mater. (photo, Eric Hylden, Grand Forks Herald)

Al "Keys" Purpur maintained the ice and ran the Winter Sports Building, long before the Zamboni was invented. (photo courtesy of Purpur family)

Grand Forks (N.D.) Central graduate Jeff Panzer led the nation in scoring in the 2000-2001 season with 81 points. He also earned first-team All-America honors for the second year in a row, and he tied for second in the voting for the Hobey Baker Memorial Award as the nation's best player.

Schepp, the support staff at UND is as good as the product on the ice.

There are many others, too, who made contributions to the program over the years, including longtime sports information director Lee Bohnet, who preserved much of the early Sioux history.

The medical staff has made remarkable contributions — both with their skill and in other ways. Dr. Ralph Leigh, and later his son, Jim Leigh, served as team doctors and helped pay for UND's training and medical facilities.

The contributions of Paul Bridston of Grand Forks shouldn't be forgotten, either. He funded the All-America wall display, featuring photographs of every Sioux All-American, and the jersey displays in the arena. He also paid for the sculpture of the hockey player that stands outside old Engelstad Arena to greet fan and foe alike.

The Morris Goddard family from Thief River Falls, Minn., provided funding for the display honoring the late Terry Casey, the former Sioux star killed in an automobile accident.

What's remarkable is how many of these unheralded people have been associated with Sioux hockey for many years. Like the players who skated for the Sioux, loyalty runs deep off the ice, too.

A good friend/ *Ralph Engelstad*

Ralph Engelstad (above), a Thief River Falls, Minn., native who played goalie at UND from 1948 to 1950, later made his fortune through real estate and construction, primarily in the Las Vegas, Nev., area. Perhaps UND hockey's biggest fan, Engelstad built the new arena at UND that bears his name. He eventually will donate it to the school. The Grand Forks (N.D.) Herald asked him to write about his passion for UND and Fighting Sioux hockey. On these two pages is his story. (photo, Chuck Kimmerle, Grand Forks Herald)

Why do I have the respect that I do for UND, the UND hockey team and the Fighting Sioux name? It's very simple.

While working during the summer of 1948 unloading boxcars with professor Ben Gustafson of UND, it was he who talked me into attending UND and arranged everything.

I came from a family that could not afford to send me to college and, if it hadn't been for professor Gustafson and the Fighting Sioux hockey team, I most likely would not have gotten an education, nor would I be where I am today.

The opportunity to go to school was a gift of immeasurable proportions that UND gave to me. Life teaches you that it is neither right nor just to forget those who have reached out and helped you along the way.

What I learned early on was that no one is going to give you anything in life; you have to work for it. As per one of my mottoes, "No dream comes true until you wake up and go to work." I can recall those memorable days as a student, the UND Fighting Sioux team loyalty, the team spirit and the thrill of victory when the Fighting Sioux hockey team won a hard-fought and well-earned victory.

My learning experience and dedication to the Fighting Sioux tradition provided the format for that road of achievement, which I often express in my other motto, being "the harder I work, the luckier I get."

It had been my desire to return to UND, the Fighting Sioux hockey team, Grand Forks and the state of North Dakota that which had been extended to me in my youth. I had made many smaller donations to the Fighting Sioux hockey team and UND through the years, but not to the extent I wished.

The devastation and trauma in Grand Forks caused by the disastrous flood and fire of 1997 created an urgency within me to do my part to help in the community's recovery. In reaction, I wanted to establish a meaningful response that would lend itself not only to providing employment and income for the area but to draw interest and revenue for the

Ralph Engelstad, a native of Thief River Falls, Minn., played goalie at UND from 1948 to 1950. He played in 14 games over the two seasons, finishing with a career goals-against average of 4.14. (photo, UND Athletics)

UND Fighting Sioux hockey team, UND, Grand Forks and the state of North Dakota.

Maintaining this prospective, in conjunction with my love for hockey, I envisioned a state-of-the-art, multipurpose sports center that would encompass those needs and interests. I wanted to create a hockey arena that would stand as a benchmark and bring additional pride to the university and its hockey team, the city and the state.

The design of the Ralph Engelstad Arena, with its engineered capabilities, is to draw the attention of the NCAA and sports fans everywhere. It also will serve as a magnet for recruiting athletes, students and faculty and give people a source of pride.

Historically, a successful comprehensive athletic program enhances a university's position and recognition.

By virtue of its presence, the Ralph Engelstad Arena will stand as a symbol for all UND students to exercise their still-to-be-tapped potential, which lies within their unrealized individualities. I wish this testament of success in giving from a UND alumnus will serve as a vehicle to encourage hope, pride, self-esteem and motivation for all students from all walks of life. To have a student identify with the meaning and intent of the Fighting Sioux, exemplified by the Ralph Engelstad Arena, will encourage involvement and participation in that tradition. This arena will be a constant reminder to students to contribute when and where they may, during life, in recognition of those people, places and events they hold near and dear.

Hopefully, the Ralph Engelstad Arena will inspire future alumni to follow that treasured tradition of giving and to follow in the footsteps of many who have sacrificed for and given to their alma mater, UND.

Many of the principles which I have adopted over the years I learned while going to UND and while a goalie for the Fighting Sioux hockey team. Interlocked with this attribution is the will not to abandon a responsibility for expressing appreciation to a time-honored title and the recognized majestic symbol of a 70-year historically placed tradition, the Fighting Sioux.

The modern-day relentless demolition and ridicule of admirable traditions have left people with little solid good to cling to in history. Those who frequent that street for the sake of destruction fail to recognize that traditions are a vital social value.

Tradition is that gentle fabric woven through time and experience, tediously implemented and practiced through a comprehensive set of crucial, individual contributions, generating meaning, character and identity to one and all. The Fighting Sioux logo, the Indian head symbol, the Fighting Sioux uniforms, the aura of the Fighting Sioux tradition and spirit of being a Fighting Sioux are of a lasting value and of immeasurable significance to our past, present and future.

Fight on Fighting Sioux,
Ralph Engelstad

President Ronald Reagan is presented with a Fighting Sioux hockey jersey on his 1986 visit to Grand Forks. (photo, Jackie Lorentz, Grand Forks Herald)

Skaters	Years	Pos.	Games	G/A/P	Pen./Min.	Hometown
A...						
Terry Abram	'66-69	D	90	10-54-64	60/139	So. St. Paul, Minn.
Earl Anderson	'69-73	W	134	69-76-145	29/58	Roseau, Minn.
James Archibald	'81-85	W	154	75-69-144	248/540	Craik, Sask.
Peter Armbrust	'96-00	W	154	21-29-50	47/121	Edina, Minn.
Joe Armbruster	'56-58	W	50	17-9-26	7/22	Fort Frances, Ont.
Dean Arnett	'77-78	W	7	1-1-2	2/4	Pilot Mound, Man.
Mark Arnett	'76-77	D	10	0-0-0	1/2	Pilot Mound, Man.
B...						
Roger Bamburak	'66-69	W	91	43-24-67	18/36	Winnipeg, Man.
Dean Barsness	'80-84	C	134	30-44-74	12/24	Grand Forks, N.D.
Robert Bartlett	'61-63	W	57	24-35-59	26/65	Edmonton, Alta.
Wade Bartley	'88-89	D	32	1-1-2	4/8	Dauphin, Man.
Murray Baron	'86-89	D	122	7-26-33	116/249	Kamloops, B.C.
Michael Baumgartner	'68-71	D	92	17-23-40	21/53	Roseau, Minn.
Ryan Bayda	'99-	W	90	42-57-99	39/78	Saskatoon, Sask.
Darren Bear	'91-94	D	100	4-16-20	51/105	Hodgson, Man.
Marcel Beaulieu	'52-54	W	33	6-3-9	5/10	Emerson, Man.
Bradley Becker	'73-77	W	143	66-57-123	67/180	Edina, Minn.
Garfield Beckstead	'57-61	W	18	1-1-2	1/2	Emerson, Man.
Robert Began	'56-59	C/D	84	12-8-20	7/14	Eveleth, Minn.
Thomas Benson	'84-88	D	159	4-45-49	129/277	Victoria, B.C.
Perry Berezan	'83-85	C	85	51-59-110	29/61	Edmonton, Alta.
Mark Berge	'76-78, '80-81	D	107	7-24-31	39/78	Grand Forks, N.D.
Bradley Berry	'83-86	D	112	12-62-74	30/60	Bashaw, Alta.
Sean Beswick	'92-95	F	96	22-13-35	30/90	Sparwood, B.C.
Jason Blake	'96-99	C	119	71-100-171	68/155	Moorhead, Minn.
Joe Blake	'96-98	D	48	1-4-5	10/20	Champlin, Minn.
Brent Bobyck	'86-90	C	159	45-60-105	54/122	Regina, Sask.
Bradley Bombardir	'90-94	D	144	19-52-71	68/144	Powell River, B.C.
Joby Bond	'90-94	F	30	1-2-3	9/26	Winnipeg, Man.
William Boone	'53-55	W	55	14-12-26	10/23	South Burnaby, B.C.
William Borlase	'61-64	D	37	3-5-8	18/36	Fort Frances, Ont.
Raymond Bostrom	'46-47	D	10	0-2-2	3/6	Grand Forks, N.D.
Jeffrey Bowen	'83-87	W	94	16-14-30	38/84	East Grand Forks, Minn.
David Bragnalo	'69-72	W	96	24-57-81	14/28	Thunder Bay, Ont.
Gary Brandt	'66-68	D	54	5-11-16	14/28	Salol, Minn.
Jeffrey Bredahl	'82-84	W	21	1-4-5	5/10	Minot, N.D.
Daniel Brennan	'80-84	W	155	50-75-125	113/240	Dawson Creek, B.C.
Michael Brickey	'87-88	W	16	2-1-3	5/10	Port Huron, Mich.
Lee Brodeur	'84-85	W	13	0-2-2	3/6	Grafton, N.D.
Thomas Brown	'74-75	D	34	1-5-6	8/19	Prince Albert, Sask.
Julian Brunetta	'56-59	D	77	8-20-28	31/62	Fort Frances, Ont.
Walter Bryduck	'53-54	W	1	1-1-2	1/2	Williams, Minn.
Jesse Bull	'95-99	F	126	36-46-82	35/70	Faribault, Minn.
Thomas Buran	'47-48	W	4	0-1-1	0/0	Roseau, Minn.
Mike Burggraf	'75-79	C	151	52-102-154	111/236	Roseau, Minn.
Frank Burggraf	'78-82	C/W	130	16-29-45	47/94	Roseau, Minn.
Richard Burns	'52-53	W	14	9-5-14	7/14	Stoneham, Mass.
James Burt	'90-92	D	37	1-2-3	14/28	Delta, B.C.
Derrick Byfuglien	'00-01	D	6	0-1-1	1/2	Roseau, Minn.
C...						
James Cahoon	'69-73	C	121	56-92-148	35/70	Melville, Sask.
Adam Calder	'95-99	C/W	141	38-69-107	102/215	Portage la Prairie, Man.
Gregory Cameron	'69-72	W	93	29-33-62	19/38	Souris, Man.
Brandon Carlson	'95-96	F	7	1-2-3	4/16	Anchorage, Alaska
Robert Caouette	'60-61	C	14	0-1-1	3/6	Crookston, Minn.
Dunstan Carroll	'79-83	C	156	59-60-119	48/115	Charlottetown, P.E.I.
Terry Casey	'63-66	C/W	88	57-61-118	7/14	Great Falls, Mont.

Peter Armbrust

Mark Arnett

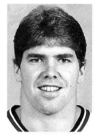
Jeff Bowen

Jim Cahoon

Dusty Carroll

James "Rick" Clubbe

Bob DePiero

Justin Duberman

Granger Evans

Glen Fester

Skaters	Years	Pos.	Games	G/A/P	Pen./Min.	Hometown
Mike Castellano	'54-57	C/W	85	32-43-75	11/22	Eveleth, Minn.
Paul Chadwick	'77-81	W	154	30-49-79	108/259	Williams Lake, B.C.
James Charlesworth	'68-71	W	87	20-29-49	18/36	Grand Forks, N.D.
Ben Cherski	'51-55	W	100	131-57-188	29/66	Edmonton, Alta.
George Chigol	'61-64	W	83	31-27-58	17/42	Flin Flon, Man.
Marcus Chorney	'77-81	D	153	24-94-118	132/278	Thunder Bay, Ont.
David Christian	'77-79	C	78	30-40-70	18/36	Warroad, Minn.
Edward Christian	'80-84	W	120	12-20-32	48/104	Warroad, Minn.
Gordon Christian	'47-50	C	59	62-43-105	23/46	Warroad, Minn.
Rodney Christensen	'67-69	W	54	10-13-23	5/10	International Falls, Minn.
William Claviter	'83-87	C/W	107	14-25-39	29/58	Virginia, Minn.
James "Rick" Clubbe	'72-76	C/W	135	37-56-93	55/151	Toronto, Ont.
David Colborne	'76-77	W	14	7-11-18	28/72	Calgary, Alta.
Wesley Cole	'47-48	W	16	8-6-14	3/6	Warroad, Minn.
Bradley Colehour	'70-73	C/W	43	3-2-5	6/12	Minneapolis, Minn.
William Colpitts	'59-61	W/C	61	36-54-90	9/18	Winnipeg, Man.
Mike Commodore	'97-00	D	106	10-20-30	151/382	Fort Saskatchewan, Alta.
Bradford Cox	'76-80	D	156	21-102-123	67/158	Lethbridge, Alta.
Kelly Cross	'70-73	W/C	78	17-30-47	5/10	Flin Flon, Man.
Donald Crough	'57-58	D	31	2-9-12	17/42	St. Albert, Alta.
James Cruise	'72-74	C	39	4-11-15	6/12	Dauphin, Man.
Jerome Culbertson	'54-57	D	83	8-22-30	45/117	Duluth, Minn.

D...

Dean Dachyshyn	'79-83	W	125	31-35-66	135/289	Devon, Alta.
Lee Davidson	'86-90	C	167	80-122-202	115/265	Winnipeg, Man.
Roy Davidson	'63-66	D	85	16-32-48	75/161	Winnipeg, Man.
Brad DeFauw	'96-00	W	150	40-38-78	86/189	Apple Valley, Minn.
Joseph Delure	'73-77	W	111	38-51-89	36/88	Calgary, Alta.
Terrence Dennis	'73-75	C	68	18-25-43	29/98	Vancouver, B.C.
Brian DePiero	'69-72	C	98	42-52-96	14/28	Thunder Bay, Ont.
Robert DePiero	'73-77	C/D	138	38-66-104	55/113	Thunder Bay, Ont.
George Dickinson	'48-51	W	61	32-45-77	20/40	Warroad, Minn.
Carmelo "Dan" DiFuria	'51-52	D	5	0-0-0	4/16	Stoneham, Mass.
James Dixon	'63-65	W	38	6-6-12	2/4	Winnipeg, Man.
Larry Dobson	'66-69	W	90	24-36-60	18/44	Flin Flon, Man.
David Donnelly	'81-83	W	72	28-31-59	61/144	Edmonton, Alta.
John Donovan	'46-47	D	12	1-1-2	1/2	St. Paul, Minn.
Wes Dorey	'97-01	W	140	47-52-99	36/72	Edmonton, Alta.
Robert Dorsher	'46-51	D	47	9-8-17	20/40	Grand Forks, N.D.
James Doyle	'47-48	W	11	1-2-3	1/2	Thief River Falls, Minn.
Daryl Drader	'72-76	D	119	16-42-58	36/88	Estevan, Sask.
Larry Drader	'72-75	W/C	96	34-40-74	32/72	Estevan, Sask.
Scott Dub	'84-88	W	151	37-34-71	124/263	Pisek, N.D.
Justin Duberman	'88-92	W	159	49-56-105	108/255	Highland Park, Ill.
Robert Duncan	'68-71	C/W	88	32-44-76	68/160	Calgary, Alta.
Hugh "Tom" Dunn	'66-68	C	48	13-15-28	9/18	Fort St. John, B.C.
Travis Dunn	'78-80	D	62	0-13-13	26/52	Winnipeg, Man.
Robert Dunsworth	'51-54	D	72	8-22-30	23/54	Edmonton, Alta.
Darryl Durgin	'55-56	W	10	1-4-5	0/0	Thief River Falls, Minn.
Ernest Dyda	'61-63	W/C	58	25-30-55	7/14	Norquay, Sask.

E...

Cary Eades	'78-82	W	144	85-79-164	111/128	Burnaby, B.C.
Neil Eisenhut	'87-91	W	148	65-83-148	37/90	Osoyoos, B.C.
Gaylord Elliott	'50-53	W	16	0-0-2	3/6	Minneapolis, Minn.
Granger Evans	'61-64	W/D	46	9-10-19	9/21	Rose Valley, Sask.
Thomas Evans	'73-75	W/D	70	22-24-46	21/42	Detroit Lakes, Minn.

F...

Glen Fester	'80-83	D	82	1-20-21	29/58	Vernon, B.C.

124

Skaters	Years	Pos.	Games	G/A/P	Pen./Min.	Hometown
James Flannery	'46-47	W	2	1-1-2	0/0	Jamestown, N.D.
Steven Fischer	'73-74	D	18	1-0-1	1/2	St. Paul, Minn.
Rick Forst	'84-88	W	90	14-11-25	32/64	Esterhazy, Sask.
Darryn Fossand	'89-91	D	91	4-12-16	22/44	Bemidji, Minn.
Michael Furlong	'65-68	W/D	88	17-22-39	47/84	Dryden, Ont.
Quinn Fylling	'00-01	F	42	4-3-7	7/25	Minot, N.D.

Steve Fischer

G...

John Gasparini	'65-68	C	88	12-37-49	40/80	Fort Frances, Ont.
Steven Gasparini	'72-73	W	23	4-5-9	7/14	Fort Frances, Ont.
David Gawley	'73-75	W	69	11-14-25	11/22	Regina, Sask.
Peter Gazley	'58-59	D	10	0-1-4	6/15	Red Deer, Alta.
Ronald Geatz	'53-56	W/C	70	25-22-47	16/35	Grand Forks, N.D.
Greg Geldart	'88-89	D	1	0-0-0	0/0	Edmonton, Alta.
David Geving	'74-76	D	77	15-47-62	45/90	Minneapolis, Minn.
Kenneth Gibb	'71-75	D/W	117	12-28-40	56/116	Stratford, Ont.
Mac Gibbs	'55-56	D	4	0-1-1	0/0	Norwood, Man.
James Gliniany	'75-78	C	97	10-14-24	6/12	Minneapolis, Minn.
Thomas Goddard	'73-77	W	141	40-59-99	44/102	Thief River Falls, Minn.
George Goodacre	'60-63	D	66	7-36-43	42/92	Red Deer, Alta.
Roger Goodman	'51-54	D	72	9-23-32	13/29	Winnipeg, Man.
Lee Goren	'97-00	W	111	66-61-127	44/88	Winnipeg, Man.
Chris Gotziaman	'90-94	F	146	38-28-66	75/152	Roseau, Minn.
Archie Graham	'46-47	C	12	0-1-1	2/4	Grand Forks, N.D.
George Gratton	'58-61	G/W	71	1-0-1	2/4	Toronto, Ont.
John Gray	'59-62	D	86	12-10-22	14/28	Winnipeg, Man.
Warren Gregg	'60-62	G	8	0-0-0	2/4	Winnipeg, Man.
Dean "Dino" Grillo	'92-94	F	66	18-18-36	14/28	Warroad, Minn.
Robert Grina	'46-49	F	35	25-16-41	2/4	Grand Forks, N.D.
Wayne Gurba	'62-64	W/C	57	27-31-58	19/41	Flin Flon, Man.

Chris Gotziaman

Dean "Dino" Grillo

H...

Duane Hagness	'46-47	W	13	8-5-13	4/13	Grand Forks, N.D.
David Hakstol	'89-92	D	107	10-36-46	77/191	Red Deer, Alta.
David Hale	'00-	D	44	4-5-9	37/77	Colorado Springs, Colo.
Ryan Hale	'99-	F	48	5-12-17	15/30	Colorado Springs, Colo.
Bernard Haley	'58-61	W	80	16-23-39	20/63	Edmonton, Alta.
Trevor Hammer	'97-01	D	152	9/44/53	43/97	Roseau, Minn.
Alan Hangsleben	'71-74	D/W	106	37-55-92	88/182	Warroad, Minn.
Kenneth Hankerson	'66-68	D	21	1-2-3	4/8	Grand Forks, N.D.
James Hannesson	'54-57	W	73	22-40-62	32/78	St. Boniface, Man.
John Hanson	'88-89	F	23	2-4-6	9/18	Eagan, Minn.
Robert Harris	'56-57	W	6	2-0-2	2/4	St. Etienmede Luzon, Quebec
Adrian Hasbargen	'99-	F/D	9	2-4-6	9/18	Warroad, Minn.
Albert Hausauer	'46-47	D	10	1-1-2	4/8	Jamestown, N.D.
James Healey	'46-47	W	12	4-6-10	7/14	Grand Forks, N.D.
John Healey	'46-47	C	13	10-5-15	6/12	Grand Forks, N.D.
Robert Hegraness	'46-47	W	13	2-2-4	3/6	Grand Forks, N.D.
Robert Helgeland	'55-57	D/W	41	2-3-5	12/27	Thief River Falls, Minn.
Matt Henderson	'94-98	W/C	135	48-44-92	84/195	White Bear Lake, Minn.
Alan Henry	'69-73	D	132	16-47-63	130/274	Falconbridge, Ont.
Jason Herter	'88-91	D	118	30-89-119	77/154	Halford, Sask.
Dennis Hextall	'64-66	W/C	63	36-65-101	27/63	Poplar Point, Man.
William Himmelright	'75-79	D	152	28-121-149	105/218	Bemidji, Minn.
David Hoogsteen	'95-99	W	140	68-89-157	29/58	Thunder Bay, Ont.
Kevin Hoogsteen	'93-97	F	148	50-60-110	70/175	Thunder Bay, Ont.
Tarek Howard	'83-87	D	112	4-24-28	47/97	Olds, Alta.
Corey Howe	'91-93	D	65	2-10-12	43/92	Roseau, Minn.
Anthony Hrkac	'84-85, 86-87	C	84	64-106-170	29/64	Thunder Bay, Ont.
Brett Hryniuk	'91-95	F	134	26-21-47	66/153	Calgary, Alta.
David Hudson	'67-70	C/D	92	40-33-73	21/50	St. Thomas, Ont.

Matt Henderson

Corey Howe

Mark Huglen

Corey Johnson

David Kath

Scott Kleven

Roger Lamoureux

Skaters	Years	Pos.	Games	G/A/P	Pen./Min.	Hometown
Mark Huglen	'83-84	W	29	1-7-8	5/10	Roseau, Minn.

I...

Thomas Iannone	'64-66	W	62	27-28-55	11/22	Flin Flon, Man.

J...

Dane Jackson	'89-92	W	120	55-39-94	90/216	Castlegar, B.C.
Donald Bruce Jackson	'65-66	W	21	1-3-4	2/4	Winnipeg, Man.
David Janaway	'64-67	W	90	25-30-55	24/48	Portage LaPrairie, Man.
Mark Jeffries	'71-72	W	13	0-0-1	3/6	Hopkins, Minn.
Chris Jensen	'82-86	W	131	77-95-172	123/261	Salmon Arm, B.C.
Waldon Jensen	'50-51	W	4	0-0-0	1/2	Grand Forks, N.D.
Arthur Jerome	'60-61	W	21	1-5-6	4/8	Devils Lake, N.D.
Kenneth Johannson	'50-53	C	71	54-85-139	18/55	Edmonton, Alta.
Chad Johnson	'90-93	F	95	6-16-22	52/118	Grand Forks, N.D.
Corey Johnson	'92-96	F	139	14-23-37	47/105	Thunder Bay, Ont.
Dennis Johnson	'70-73	W	82	23-37-60	20/40	Grand Forks, N.D.
Gregory Johnson	'89-93	C	155	74-198-272	29/74	Thunder Bay, Ont.
John Johnson	'46-47	W	12	1-0-1	6/18	Grand Forks, N.D.
Robert Johnson	'50-51	W	24	15-5-20	9/21	Minneapolis, Minn.
Milton "Prince" Johnson	'47-50	W	39	49-21-70	15/30	Webster, S.D.
Ross Johnson	'88-90	W	72	11-16-27	17/34	Rochester, Minn.
Russel "Buzz" Johnson	'47-50	C/W	38	35-31-66	23/51	Webster, S.D.
Ryan Johnson	'94-96	C/W	59	8-39-47	21/53	Thunder Bay, Ont.
Steven Johnson	'84-88	W/C	153	70-121-191	48/99	Grand Forks, N.D.
Douglas Johnston	'67-70	W	81	26-24-50	61/133	Harriston, Ont.
Robert Joyce	'84-87	W	127	101-81-182	46/92	Winnipeg, Man.

K...

Gary Kaiser	'86-87	D	9	0-1-1	9/18	Fargo, N.D.
Ian Kallay	'95-97	W	76	39-45-84	17/34	Whitecourt, Alta.
David Kartio	'66-69	W	91	58-36-94	14/31	Sault Ste. Marie, Ont.
David Kath	'74-75	C	9	2-0-2	2/4	Roseville, Minn.
Gerald Kell	'63-65	W/C	58	38-42-80	22/56	Kildonan, Man.
Pat Kenny	'98-00	W	9	0-0-0	0/0	Edmonton, Alta.
Ian Kidd	'85-87	D	84	19-63-82	60/123	Gresham, Ore.
William Killian	'46-47	W	13	1-1-2	1/2	Seattle, Wash.
Ronald King	'57-60	W	94	23-31-54	33/74	Fort Frances, Ont.
Scott Kirton	'91-95	F	131	20-48-68	105/282	Elmvale, Ont.
Scott Kleven	'70-72	W	10	1-0-1	0/0	Red Lake Falls, Minn.
Glen Klotz	'82-86	W	140	18-87-105	60/126	Edmonton, Alta.
James Knauf	'55-56	C/W	22	1-0-1	6/20	Grand Forks, N.D.
John Knauf	'56-57	W	8	0-0-0	1/2	Grand Forks, N.D.
Scott Koberinski	'85-89	C	160	48-88-136	57/122	North Battleford, Sask.
Robert Kochevar	'55-56	C	20	3-3-6	1/2	Eveleth, Minn.
Joey Kompon	'73-75	W	65	13-25-38	17/42	Thunder Bay, Ont.
Mickey Krampotich	'83-87	C/W	155	64-72-136	29/58	Hibbing, Minn.
Robert Krumholz	'47-52	W	79	47-42-89	31/76	Hallock, Minn.
Paul Kryworuchka	'77-78	W	36	5-9-14	15/30	Prince Albert, Sask.

L...

Jerry Lafond	'64-67	D	90	13-35-48	15/46	Dawson Creek, B.C.
Guy LaFrance	'57-60	C/D	93	33-60-93	37/93	Fort Frances, Ont.
Michael LaMoine	'85-89	D	140	8-40-48	65/131	Grand Forks, N.D.
Roger Lamoureux	'73-77	C/W	144	48-85-133	67/134	Calgary, Alta.
Lowell Lanigan	'68-69	D	26	0-7-7	11/22	Regina, Sask.
Kent Langlie	'72-73	D	6	0-1-1	4/8	Roseau, Minn.
Bartley Larson	'58-61	W	85	12-17-29	15/46	Minneapolis, Minn.
Jonathan Larson	'89-93	D	94	3-10-13	25/58	Roseau, Minn.
Robert Law	'71-73	W	68	13-20-33	12/24	Fort Frances, Ont.
Robert Lawson	'72-73	D	34	5-12-17	15/38	Taconite, Minn.
James Leigh	'46-47	W	13	2-2-4	1/2	Grand Forks, N.D.

Skaters	Years	Pos.	Games	G/A/P	Pen./Min.	Hometown
Chris Leinweber	'99-	D	79	1-14-15	24/48	Calgary, Alta.
Robert Lillo	'64-67	W	83	19-28-47	9/18	Roseau, Minn.
Dane Litke	'93-97	D	136	7-62-69	25/50	Beausejour, Man.
Tim Loven	'82-85	D	80	1-18-19	13/26	Grand Forks, N.D.
Craig Ludwig	'79-82	D	114	10-42-52	71/150	Eagle River, Wis.
Durwood Lund	'50-53	W	63	36-33-69	11/22	Thief River Falls, Minn.
Bryan Lundbohm	'98-01	W	122	56-68-124	28/56	Roseau, Minn.
David Lundbohm	'00-	W	39	9-10-19	14/28	Roseau, Minn.
Michael Lundbohm	'69-72	C	72	9-7-16	4/8	Roseau, Minn.
Michael Lundby	'70-73	D/W	81	12-29-41	16/35	Grand Forks, N.D.
Ralph Lyndon	'57-60	D	74	11-26-37	48/99	Winnipeg, Man.
Gary Lyons	'66-68	W	49	3-9-12	14/31	Baudette, Minn.

Craig Ludwig

M...

Skaters	Years	Pos.	Games	G/A/P	Pen./Min.	Hometown
Peter MacKenzie	'64-67	D	92	3-18-21	20/40	Winnipeg, Man.
Troy Magnuson	'79-82	W	65	10-10-20	15/33	Chanhassen, Minn.
Zdenek "Stan" Marek	'50-51	C	24	15-19-34	7/22	Prostejor, Czechoslovakia
John Marks	'67-70	D	92	14-46-60	44/88	Winnipeg, Man.
Erwin Martens	'76-80	W	151	49-50-99	56/110	Cartwright, Man.
Calvin Marvin	'47-50	D	55	0-10-10	16/32	Warroad, Minn.
Conway Marvin	'78-80	D	40	0-8-8	16/32	Warroad, Minn.
David Marvin	'87-91	D	159	12-65-77	75/116	Warroad, Minn.
Randolph Marvin	'73-78	D	121	5-18-23	135/302	Warroad, Minn.
Jack Matheson	'61-63	W	54	14-16-30	27/57	Brandon, Man.
John Mathews	'67-68	W	4	0-1-1	0/0	Winnipeg, Man.
Kevin Maxwell	'78-79	D	42	31-51-82	35/79	Chilliwack, B.C.
Randy Maxwell	'82-83	C	26	4-5-9	5/10	Chilliwack, B.C.
Robert May	'49-51	D	47	2-3-5	29/58	Sprague, Man.
David Mazur	'63-65	W/C	58	21-39-60	14/28	Dauphin, Man.
Chad Mazurak	'98-	D	109	14-36-50	70/156	Regina, Sask.
Robert "Mike" McCormick	'87-90	D	60	5-4-9	23/50	Lynnwood, Wash.
Shane McFarlane	'87-90	C	81	4-7-11	14/28	Warroad, Minn.
Daniel McKinnon	'47-50	D	61	7-8-15	25/53	Williams, Minn.
Kevin McKinnon	'89-90, 91-94	F	118	36-33-69	38/84	Carman, Man.
Paul McKinnon	'47-50	D	37	9-7-16	19/38	Williams, Minn.
Alan McLean	'61-63	C/W	58	37-53-90	25/72	New Westminster, B.C.
Jeffrey McLean	'87-88, 89-92	W	163	56-88-144	55/118	Port Moody, B.C.
Charles Medved	'47-50	C	41	45-50-95	15/30	Crookston, Minn.
Harlen Meek	'55-56	W	22	0-1-1	1/10	Warroad, Minn.
David Merrifield	'60-63	C	76	45-59-104	28/72	Thunder Bay, Ont.
Leslie Merrifield	'57-60	W	93	24-41-65	40/109	Thunder Bay, Ont.
James Meuwissen	'82-84	D	30	2-8-10	11/22	Minneapolis, Minn.
Rob Mihulka	'75-79	D/W	152	40-62-102	53/106	Grafton, N.D.
Arthur Miller	'57-60	W	93	65-52-117	28/64	Moose Jaw, Sask.
Gerald Miller	'69-73	W	129	46-42-88	62/151	Moose Jaw, Sask.
Timothy Mishler	'82-83	W	18	4-4-8	0/0	East Grand Forks, Minn.
Darcy Mitani	'92-96	F	140	55-57-112	78/162	Dryden, Ont.
Matthew Morelli	'87-91	W	74	7-3-10	6/12	Minot, N.D.
Reginald Morelli	'57-60	C	85	60-72-132	13/34	Hamilton, Ont.
Frank Morgan	'51-52	W	23	1-1-2	6/12	West Haven, Conn.
Carl Morken	'50-51	D	10	0-0-0	2/4	Grand Forks, N.D.
John Morrison	'56-57	D	6	0-0-0	2/4	Selkirk, Man.
Robert Mowris	'46-47	W	13	0-1-1	1/2	Thief River Falls, Minn.
Robert Munro	'66-69	C	81	38-71-109	23/56	Geraldton, Ont.
Aaron Murphy	'97-98	W	2	0-0-0	3/6	Grand Rapids, Minn.
Curtis Murphy	'94-98	D	153	32-86-118	88/196	Kerrobert, Sask.
Keith Murphy	'92-95	F	109	20-10-30	24/59	Kerrobert, Sask.
Paul Murphy	'98-01	D/W	70	2-19-21	11/33	Manvel, N.D.
Troy Murray	'80-82	C	80	55-74-129	45/90	St. Albert, Alta.
Barry Myers	'54-55	D	10	1-2-3	6/12	Winnipeg Man.
Rick Myers	'75-80	W	126	45-61-106	25/51	East Grand Forks, Minn.

Kevin Maxwell

Darcy Mitani

Bob Munro

Keith Murphy

Tim O'Keefe

James Patrick

Tom Philion

Gary Purpur

Donny Riendeau

Skaters	Years	Pos.	Games	G/A/P	Pen./Min.	Hometown
John Myhre	'75-76	D	7	0-1-1	0/0	Minneapolis, Minn

N...

Skaters	Years	Pos.	Games	G/A/P	Pen./Min.	Hometown
Perry Nakonechny	'83-87	W	144	27-38-65	54/108	Dauphin, Man.
Nick Naumenko	'92-96	D	146	38-102-140	81/178	Chicago, Ill.
Michael Neitzke	'75-80	W	74	15-15-30	17/34	Detroit Lakes, Minn.
Jay Ness	'82-85	D	19	0-0-0	4/8	Roseau, Minn.
John Noah	'47-51	D/C	67	29-44-73	15/30	Crookston, Minn.
Scott Nieland	'75-76	D	32	2-10-12	11/22	Edina, Minn.
Jeffrey Norby	'76-77	D	17	1-3-4	4/8	Detroit Lakes, Minn.
Orval "Ossie" Nord	'46-47	W	12	2-2-4	0/0	Detroit Lakes, Minn.
Todd Norman	'84-86	W	61	14-7-21	35/78	St. Paul, Minn.
Jason Notermann	'99-	F	85	18-25-43	28/78	Rochester, Minn.
John Novak	'51-54	D	47	5-21-26	30/63	Winnipeg, Man.

O...

Skaters	Years	Pos.	Games	G/A/P	Pen./Min.	Hometown
Tim O'Connell	'96-00	D	115	1-16-17	47/132	Grand Forks, N.D.
Terry Ogden	'65-68	D	82	4-24-28	27/57	Fort Frances, Ont.
Timothy O'Keefe	'68-71	D/C	75	4-12-16	7/14	Grand Forks, N.D.
Pat O'Leary	'00-	F	33	4-3-7	9/29	Fargo, N.D.
Arley Olson	'80-81	D	28	1-1-2	5/10	Eatonia, Sask.
Jarrod Olson	'91-95	D	82	4-7-10	27/54	Minot, N.D.
Lars Oxholm	'91-93	D	37	1-7-8	30/68	Herning, Denmark

P...

Skaters	Years	Pos.	Games	G/A/P	Pen./Min.	Hometown
Anthony Palmiscno	'72-74	W	15	3-2-5	2/4	Grand Forks, N.D.
Steven Palmiscno	'80-84	W	85	20-32-52	18/36	Grand Forks, N.D.
Tyler Palmiscno	'00-	F	30	3-2-5	3/6	East Grand Forks, Minn.
Jay Panzer	'95-99	W	143	58-86-144	25/58	Grand Forks, N.D.
Jeff Panzer	'97-01	C	164	80-148-228	38/76	Grand Forks, N.D.
Terry Paoletti	'55-56	D	7	0-0-0	2/4	Eveleth, Minn.
Grant Paranica	'85-89	W	129	42-44-86	80/162	N. Battleford, Sask.
Russell Parent	'86-90	D	162	24-115-139	100/225	Winnipeg, Man.
Malcolm Parks	'83-87	W	159	39-52-91	80/171	Edmonton, Alta.
Brad Pascall	'88-92	D	114	2-20-22	126/264	Coquitham, B.C.
Stanley Paschke	'56-59	W	92	24-29-53	9/24	Grand Forks, N.D.
Daniel Passolt	'74-75	C	4	0-0-0	2/4	St. Louis Park, Minn.
James Patrick	'81-83	D	78	17-60-77	26/55	Winnipeg, Man.
Walter Pederson	'51-54	W	53	4-9-13	4/8	Greenbush, Minn.
William Perry	'58-61	W	18	0-0-0	3/9	Red Deer, Alta.
Robert Peskey	'46-47	D	13	1-2-3	7/14	St. Louis Park, Minn.
Tom Philion	'95-99	C/W	69	8-10-18	10/20	Minot, N.D.
Robert Phillips	'48-50	W	8	1-0-1	0/0	Noyes, Minn.
Mark Pivetz	'93-97	D	145	12-38-50	95/228	Edmonton, Alta.
Joseph Poole	'56-59	C	90	42-52-94	22/47	Thief River Falls, Minn.
Mike Possin	'98-	W	23	1-0-1	12/24	St. Cloud, Minn.
Gary Purpur	'71-72	C	11	2-1-3	0/0	Grand Forks, N.D.
Kenneth Purpur	'51-54	C	72	46-71-117	27/65	Grand Forks, N.D.

R...

Skaters	Years	Pos.	Games	G/A/P	Pen./Min.	Hometown
Kevin Rappana	'91-96	D	110	1-12-13	104/241	Duluth, Minn.
Jace Reed	'89-91	D	23	0-0-0	2/4	Grand Rapids, Minn.
William Reichart	'54-57	W/C	85	97-59-156	23/57	Winnipeg, Man.
Tyler Rice	'94-95, 96-97	F	46	7-13-20	43/127	Winnipeg, Man.
James Ridley	'55-58	W	88	64-71-135	50/135	Portage La Prairie, Man.
Donald Riendeau	'90-93	C	104	23-29-52	58/159	East Grand Forks, Minn.
Maurice "Sonny" Roberge	'61-64	D	72	4-15-19	28/56	Edmonton, Alta.
Travis Roche	'99-01	D	88	17-60-77	47/102	Whitecourt, Alta.
Russell Romaniuk	'88-91	W	123	93-57-150	50/116	Winnipeg, Man.
Curtis Roseborough	'59-62	D	86	10-25-35	47/97	Winnipeg, Man.

Skaters	Years	Pos.	Games	G/A/P	Pen./Min.	Hometown
Donald Ross	'61-64	D/C	89	38-48-86	31/62	Roseau, Minn.
Henry Rubert	'78-79	W	6	0-0-0	2/4	Thunder Bay, Ont.
Walter Running	'53-56	D	77	1-14-15	35/70	Fargo, N.D.
Joseph Russell	'73-75	D	67	5-9-14	14/28	Minneapolis, Minn.
Paul Rygh	'63-66	W	76	11-9-20	9/18	Roseau, Minn.

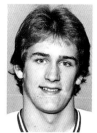

Gord Sherven

S...

Skaters	Years	Pos.	Games	G/A/P	Pen./Min.	Hometown
Scott Sandelin	'82-86	D	149	16-77-93	51/102	Hibbing, Minn.
Aaron Schneekloth	'98-	D	115	11-33-44	37/74	Calgary, Alta.
Martin Schriner	'90-94	F	145	35-64-99	192/487	Port Huron, Mich.
Scott Schroeder	'82-86	D	50	4-12-16	10/23	East Grand Forks, Minn.
Paxton Schulte	'90-91	F	38	2-4-6	12/32	Onaway, Alta.
William Selman	'60-63	D	72	1-19-20	28/56	Fort Frances, Ont.
Wilfred Shannon	'51-56	W	57	14-33-47	13/42	Winnipeg, Man.
Elwood Shell	'51-54	D/C	70	11-38-49	46/119	Edmonton, Alta.
Gordon Sherven	'81-84	W/C	92	35-51-86	18/36	Mankota, Sask.
Robert Shupe	'65-66	D	8	0-0-0	1/2	Weyburn, Sask.
Joe Silovich	'47-50	D	61	22-9-31	54/130	Eveleth, Minn.
Tim Skarperud	'99-	F	83	21-24-45	23/46	Grand Forks, N.D.
Abert Slivinski	'59-61	D	43	1-6-7	34/79	Thunder Bay, Ont.
Tim Slukynsky	'94-95	F	21	0-4-4	2/4	Portage La Prairie, Minn.
Rudolph Slupski	'54-55	D	19	0-1-1	4/8	Winnipeg, Man.
Douglas Smail	'77-80	W	113	89-106-195	84/168	Moose Jaw, Sask.
Geoff Smith	'87-88	D	51	4-13-17	24/48	Edmonton, Alta.
James "Bob" South	'46-47	W	12	0-0-0	2/4	Fargo, N.D.
Kevin Spiewak	'99-	F	83	15-29-44	32/64	Schaumburg, Ill.
John Spolar	'54-55	D	24	0-1-1	1/2	Virginia, Minn.
Peter Stasiuk	'60-63	W	79	10-13-23	21/50	Lethbridge, Alta.
William Steenson	'56-59	D	83	12-33-45	68/169	Moose Jaw, Sask.
Arnold Steeves	'62-63	W	5	0-1-1	1/2	Marathon, Ont.
Wilmot Stirrett	'62-64	W	47	11-8-19	12/24	Thunder Bay, Ont.
Donald Stokaluk	'61-64	W	65	16-14-30	8/16	Thunder Bay, Ont.
Michael Stone	'77-79, '80-82	D	161	25-74-99	116/251	Roseau, Minn.
Daniel Storsteen	'60-63	W	87	21-44-65	42/84	Devils Lake, N.D.
Jack Stoskopf	'55-57	W	8	4-5-9	2/12	Warroad, Minn.
Bob Stoyko	'64-65	C	33	19-21-40	16/32	Winnipeg, Man.
Leslie Strachan	'75-76	D	2	0-0-0	1/2	Kelowna, B.C.
Brian Strimbiski	'64-66	W	60	28-38-66	46/107	Winnipeg, Man.
James Stuart	'68-70	W	51	2-5-7	9/18	Bowden, Alta.
Chad Sturrock	'94-95	F	24	0-3-3	7/14	Stettler, Alta.
Dennis Sullivan	'48-49	W	21	2-5-7	0/0	Crookston, Minn.
William Sullivan	'47-50	W	57	23-17-40	5/10	Crookston, Minn.
John Sutherland	'61-64	D	79	8-16-24	51/118	Winnipeg, Man.
Don Swartz	'74-78	W	138	27-35-62	61/131	Grafton, N.D.
Phil Sykes	'78-82	W	161	98-90-188	42/92	Dawson Creek, B.C.

Bob Stoyko

Phil Sykes

T...

Skaters	Years	Pos.	Games	G/A/P	Pen./Min.	Hometown
Mark Taylor	'76-80	W/C	157	97-168-265	44/96	Vancouver, B.C.
Chester Tesarowski	'55-56	W	7	0-0-0	2/4	Calder, Sask.
Edward Thomlinson	'57-60	W	95	49-53-102	34/68	Sault Ste. Marie, Ont.
Stephen Thullner	'58-60	D	45	6-14-20	16/32	Winnipeg, Man.
David Tippett	'81-83	C	79	28-59-87	34/68	Prince Albert, Sask.
David Tremblay	'75-76	W	28	3-1-4	9/18	Hawkesbury, Ont.
Billy Trew	'94-96	C	67	13-23-36	12/24	Winnipeg, Man.
William Trimble	'51-54	W	32	6-5-11	5/10	Edmonton, Alta.
Robert Tuff	'66-69	W	85	27-26-53	17/50	Calgary, Alta.

Dave Tremblay

U...

Skaters	Years	Pos.	Games	G/A/P	Pen./Min.	Hometown
Jason Ulmer	'96-00	C/W	146	33-69-102	35/100	Wilcox, Sask.
Jeff Ulmer	'95-99	C/W	135	39-46-85	66/132	Wilcox, Sask.
Richard Ulvin	'63-66	D	61	7-11-18	18/36	Roseau, Minn.

Jason Ulmer

Mickey Volcan

Ken Walters

Landon Wilson

Brian Zierke

Jon Casey

Skaters	Years	Pos.	Games	G/A/P	Pen./Min.	Hometown
V...						
Garry Valk	'87-90	W	121	59-46-105	111/227	Edmonton, Alta.
Mitch Vig	'94-98	D	115	5-17-22	60/144	Bismarck, N.D.
James Vilandre	'80-81	W	16	0-1-1	2/4	Grand Forks, N.D.
Michael Volcan	'79-80	D	33	2-14-16	19/38	Edmonton, Alta.
W...						
John Wade	'53-56	C	83	30-38-68	10/20	Winnipeg, Man.
Gerald Walford	'58-61	C/W	74	26-22-48	19/41	Sudbury, Ont.
Howard Walker	'78-80	D	77	14-34-48	53/133	Grande Prairie, Alta.
Kenneth Walters	'63-65	C	25	2-1-3	2/4	Grand Forks, N.D.
Dixon Ward	'88-92	W	163	110-109-219	105/244	Leduc, Alta.
Ernest Warnock	'51-55	C/W	77	17-9-26	3/9	Wakefield, Mass.
Kenneth Wellen	'58-59	C	10	1-1-2	1/2	Roseau, Minn.
Donald L. "Blacky" White	'60-61	W	13	1-2-3	2/4	Winnipeg, Man.
Donald W. "Whitey" White	'60-62	W	29	14-14-28	11/25	Winnipeg, Man.
Glen White	'79-83	C/W	147	54-65-119	41/82	Rosetown, Sask.
William Whitsitt	'80-84	D	145	8-32-40	30/63	Bloomington, Minn.
Brad Williamson	'95-99	D	155	22-77-99	83/166	Thunder Bay, Ont.
Edgar Willems	'55-58	D	69	9-19-28	52/104	Winnipeg, Man.
Kenneth Wilkie	'50-53	W/D	56	7-5-12	16/32	Neepawa, Man.
Brian Williams	'82-86	C/W	162	71-109-180	89/192	Fargo, N.D.
James "Itts" Williams	'47-48	D	3	0-0-0	2/4	Grand Forks, N.D.
William Wilms	'63-66	W	81	33-31-64	11/30	Winnipeg, Man.
Edward Wilson	'47-51	C/W	69	22-17-39	5/10	Warroad, Minn.
Landon Wilson	'93-95	C	66	25-31-56	106/288	Eden Prairie, Minn.
Richard Wilson	'69-72	D	97	15-38-53	98/234	Prince Albert, Sask.
Murray Wing	'70-71	D	29	3-10-13	9/18	Thunder Bay, Ont.
Blaine Winters	'71-73	W	51	3-2-5	6/12	Flin Flon, Man.
Nate Wright	'00-	D	1	0-0-0	1/2	Alexandria, Minn.
Fred "Teeder" Wynne	'92-96	C	114	58-83-141	40/99	Calgary, Alta.
Y...						
Jeff Yurecko	'99-01	F	29	2-1-3	12/24	Edina, Minn.
Z...						
Richard Zaparniuk,	'76-80	C	157	60-125-185	44/98	Edmonton, Alta.
James Zavoral	'55-56	W	5	0-1-1	0/0	Thief River Falls, Minn.
Brian Zierke	'93-96	F	64	11-13-24	65/171	Brainerd, Minn.
Richard Zombo	'81-84	D	112	13-50-63	53/112	Des Plaines, Ill.

Goalies	Years	Games	GA	GAA	SVS	SV%	SO	Hometown
B...								
George Baland	'61-64	6	11	1.83	66	.866	0	Virginia, Minn.
Edward Belfour	'86-87	33.3	81	2.43	876	.915	3	Carman, Man.
Brian Blanchard	'68-69	14.7	56	3.81	374	.870	1	New Westminster, B.C.
William Borovsky	'55-56	6	38	7.60	198	.839	0	Grand Forks, N.D.
Scott Brower	'84-88	84.3	300	3.56	2,433	.890	4	Viking, Alta.
C...								
Daniel "Cory" Cadden	'90-91	3	9	3.40	78	.876	0	Leduc, Alta.
Jonathan Casey	'80-84	76.7	222	2.89	2,306	.910	3	Grand Rapids, Minn.
Tony Couture	'88-91	58.33	187	3.38	1,433	.879	0	International Falls, Minn.
Michael "Lefty" Curran	'65-68	84.3	251	2.98	2,180	.897	3	International Falls, Minn.
D...								
Timothy Delmore	'71-73	23.3	97	4.16	675	.874	0	Roseau, Minn.
Edward Derrett	'53-54	2	10	5.00	47	.825	0	Winnipeg, Man.
Christopher Dickson	'87-91	77.5	277	3.68	1,894	.872	1	Vancouver, B.C.
Melvin Donnelly	'77-80	28.3	118	4.17	857	.879	1	Fort Francis, Ont.

Goalies	Years	Games	GA	GAA	SVS	SV%	SO	Hometown
E, F...								
Jason Endres	'99-00	2	2	1.73	13	.867	0	Grand Forks, N.D.
Ralph Engelstad	'48-50	14	58	4.14	381	.868	0	Thief River Falls, Minn.
Alex Finkelstein	'51-53	44	170	3.86	1,188	.875	3	Winnipeg, Man.
Arthur Forman	'46-48	10	41	5.10	238	.850	0	Wahpeton, N.D.
G...								
Karl Goehring	'97-01	118	249	2.23	2,783	.918	15	Apple Valley, Minn.
George Gratton	'58-61	60	264	3.83	1,667	.864	1	Toronto, Ont.
Warren Gregg	'59-62	8	41	5.13	215	.811	0	Winnipeg, Man.
H, I...								
Gordon Hangsleben	'73-75	8.7	40	4.60	262	.868	0	East Grand Forks, Minn.
William Howard	'63-64	1	4	4.00	33	.892	0	Grand Forks, N.D.
Robert Iwabuchi	'78-80	46.6	131	2.81	1,087	.892	1	Edmonton, Alta.
J, K...								
Darren Jensen	'79-82	69.3	236	3.41	1,955	.894	1	Creston, B.C.
Todd Jones	'91-94	54	231	4.69	1,569	.872	0	Thunder Bay, Ont.
Billy Kriski	'72-73	2	6	3.00	36	.875	1	Winnipeg, Man.
Andy Kollar	'98-	47	119	2.71	1,127	.904	2	Winnipeg, Man.
Toby Kvalevog	'93-97	121	424	3.82	2,936	.873	2	Bemidji, Minn.
L...								
Jean Pierre Lamoureux	'79-82	30.7	102	3.40	783	.897	1	Fort Saskatchewan, Alta.
Joseph Lech	'62-65	80	223	2.79	1,838	.892	4	Glen Bain, Sask.
Jeff Lembke	'91-95	25	92	5.67	493	.843	0	Pembina, N.D.
Rudolph Lindbeck	'48-52	28	146	5.21	740	.835	0	South St. Paul, Minn.
M, N, O...								
William Maruska	'54-55	2	3	1.50	26	.900	0	St. Paul, Minn.
David Murphy	'69-73	67.7	280	4.14	1,877	.870	0	Sault Ste. Marie, Ont.
Robert Murray	'47-50	45	238	5.29	1,438	.858	1	Warroad, Minn.
James Nelson	'68-71	47	196	4.17	1,391	.876	0	Roseau, Minn.
Dudley Otto	'59-63	35	145	4.14	873	.756	9	South St. Paul, Minn.
P...								
Gerald Patterson	'46-47	5	19	3.80	150	.870	0	Rainy River, Ont.
Travis Pavlat	'95-96	2	2	1.79	22	.917	0	Sault Ste. Marie, Mich.
Robert Peabody	'57-59	40	123	3.08	803	.867	2	Grand Forks, N.D.
Craig Perry	'83-86	4.3	17	3.95	109	.865	0	Fort Frances, Ont.
Robert Peters	'57-58	11	14	1.27	205	.927	2	Fort Frances, Ont.
Steven Peters	'87-90	14.99	54	3.60	395	.880	0	Bemidji, Minn.
Kevin Powell	'92-95	29	107	4.58	653	.859	0	Columbia Heights, Minn.
S...								
Gerald Schultz	'53-55	49	193	3.94	1,408	.879	5	Edmonton, Alta.
Aaron Schweitzer	'96-98	38	97	2.99	754	.886	5	Regina, Sask.
Gary Severson	'67-69	15	69	4.60	360	.839	0	Grand Forks, N.D.
Darrell Skramstad	'63-64	4	0	0.00	0	.000	0	Devils Lake, N.D.
Ryan Sofie	'00-	1	2	4.02	7	.778	0	Baxter, Minn.
William Stankoven	'75-79	69.3	329	4.75	2,466	.881	0	Enderby, B.C.
Dale Stauss	'64-67	5	25	5.00	125	.893	0	East Grand Forks, Minn.
Greg Strome	'83-87	40	152	3.80	1,045	.873	0	Muenster, Sask.
Robert Sween	'78-79	0	0	0.00	0	.000	0	Wayzata, Minn.
V, W, Y...								
Aaron Vickar	'95-97	16	43	3.97	227	.841	0	St. Louis, Mo.
Peter Waselovich	'73-77	103.3	503	4.87	3,517	.875	2	International Falls, Minn.
Frank Watkinson	'57-58	1	7	7.00	17	.708	0	Virginia, Minn.
Thomas Yurkovich	'54-57	58	201	3.47	1,361	.875	5	Eveleth, Minn.

Bob Iwabuchi

Darren Jensen

Craig Perry

Aaron Schweitzer

Bill Stankoven

* Information for letterwinners provided by the University of North Dakota.

September 1946: The University of North Dakota hires John C. "Jamie" Jamieson as hockey coach. Jamieson, a student at the university, leads the first postwar team to a 7-6-0 overall record, playing area towns and college teams. Jamieson's 19-player squad opens the season at home Jan. 6, 1947, losing 8-1 to St. Cloud (Minn.) Teachers College.

Jan. 9, 1948: UND crashes into big-time college hockey when it stuns the Michigan Wolverines 6-5 in Ann Arbor. Strong defense and a pair of goals each from John Noah, Gordon "Ginny" Christian and Jim Medved key the big win. Noah scores the winning goal at 19:14 of the third period. Bob Murray stops 34 Michigan shots in the UND nets.

1951 to 1952: UND, a charter member of the Midwest Intercollegiate Hockey League, the forerunner of the WCHA, finishes the season with a 13-11-1 record under third-year head coach Cliff "Fido" Purpur by sweeping four games from Michigan Tech and splitting with the universities of Minnesota and Michigan.

1952 to 1953: North Dakota sprints to a 13-0 start, the best ever by a UND team, but ends the season with two losses at the University of Michigan to keep UND from its first NCAA tournament bid.

Autumn 1953: The autumn of 1953 finds the arrival of artificial ice in UND's Winter Sports Building — or the "barn" as it often was called — as Sioux hockey is growing in popularity.

Jan. 14-15, 28-29, 1954: Gerald "Spike" Schultz stones Michigan Tech with four consecutive shutouts 5-0, 5-0 at Tech and 4-0, 7-0 at UND in Western Intercollegiate Hockey League action.

March 15-16, 1958: Seven different Sioux score as UND routs Harvard 9-1 in Minneapolis in its first trip to the NCAA semifinals. WIHL opponent Denver, however, stops the Sioux 6-2 in the championship game, leaving Sioux players with unfinished business heading into the 1958-1959 season.

March 12-14, 1959: UND wins its first national championship by virtue of two action-packed 4-3 overtime thrillers at RPI in Troy, N.Y. Guy LaFrance's goal at 4:22 of overtime eliminates St. Lawrence in the semifinal game. Reg Morelli scores a pair of goals, and Art Miller and Ed Thomlinson one each in the St. Lawrence game. Morelli duplicates LaFrance's OT heroics when he scores at 4:18 of the first overtime period in the championship game against Michigan State, giving the Sioux a 4-3 win. The Spartans lead 1-0 after one period, but the Sioux go up 3-1 in the second on goals by Ralph Lyndon, Jerry Walford and Stan Paschke. State ties it late in the third, setting the stage for Morelli's dramatic shot over the sprawling Spartan goalie Joe Selinger, who records 26 saves. George Gratton stops 21 MSU shots. Morelli is tournament Most Outstanding Player.

Dec. 30, 1960: UND drops a hard-fought 4-3 decision to the touring Soviet All-Star team, the top players in the Soviet Union, when the Soviets score at 7:38 of the third period. The game marks the first time UND has met a European team and is played before

132

3,000 spectators. Dave Merrifield and Bill Colpitts give UND a 2-1 first-period lead. Donald "Whitey" White sends UND ahead 3-2 midway through the second period. George Gratton records 24 saves in the Sioux nets. The Soviet goalie has 21 stops.

March 14-16, 1963: UND tops host Boston (Mass.) College 8-2 in the semifinals of the NCAA tournament. Don Stokaluk and Pete Stasiuk each score a pair of goals, while Dave Merrifield, John Sutherland, Al McLean and Ernie Dyda score one apiece. Joe Lech makes 18 saves, while two Boston goalies record 43. UND races to a 5-2 first-period lead over Denver to win its second NCAA title on two goals by Stokaluk and McLean, Dyda and Jack Matheson. McLean, who is named tourney Most Outstanding Player, scores the winning goal at 5:01 of the second period to make it 6-5 for the Sioux. UND's Joe Lech makes only 11 saves, while Rudy Unis of Denver has 32.

March 18-20, 1965: UND loses to Boston College 4-3 at Brown University in Providence, R.I., in the first round of the NCAA tournament and then defeats host Brown 9-5 for third place.

Longtime UND timers and keepers of the penalty box John Smith (right) and the late Wendy Feist (center) keep a close eye on the damage as a University of British Columbia player is checked heavily into the boards during an exhibition game against the Sioux in the 1982-1983 season. (photo, bill alkofer, Dakota Student)

March 16, 1967: The Fighting Sioux win the WCHA and top the University of Minnesota 7-2 and Denver 3-2 in the playoffs to advance to the NCAA tournament. Cornell and goaltender Ken Dryden shut out the Sioux 1-0 in the semifinals.

March 15-16, 1968: UND beats Cornell 3-1 in the first round of the NCAA tournament in Duluth, Minn., but falls to Denver 4-0 in the title game. UND advances to the NCAA tournament by beating homestanding Michigan Tech 3-2 in a total goals series. The first game is a 0-0 deadlock, the only scoreless tie in UND history.

Dec. 21, 1968: UND edges Minnesota 5-4 in five overtimes in the final of the St. Paul Classic tournament on a Buzz Christensen goal at 2:09 of the fifth OT. The game lasts nearly five hours.

Nov. 10, 1972: UND dedicates its new $2 million Winter Sports Center by defeating Colorado College 5-4 before a capacity crowd.

March 7, 1978: John "Gino" Gasparini, a North Dakota assistant coach since 1971, is named head hockey coach. He replaces Rube Bjorkman, who announces his resignation on Jan. 4, 1978.

March 3, 1979: UND wins its first WCHA championship in 12 years by beating Minnesota on the road 4-2 under the guidance of first-year head coach Gino Gasparini.

March 23-24, 1979: UND defeats Dartmouth College 4-2 in Detroit's Olympia Stadium in the

133

semifinals of the NCAA tournament. UND uses goals from Howard Walker, Erwin Martens, Mark Taylor and Cary Eades in the victory. Minnesota edges the Sioux 4-3 in the title game. Sioux goals are scored by Bill Himmelright, Kevin Maxwell and Marc Chorney.

March 27-28, 1980: The Sioux top Dartmouth 4-1 at Providence, R.I., on four third-period goals — including two by Phil Sykes. The Sioux ride four goals by Doug Smail to a 5-2 win over Northern Michigan to win their third national championship.

March 27, 1982: The Sioux win their fourth national title by a 5-2 margin over the University of Wisconsin after third-period goals by Phil Sykes (two) and Cary Eades snap a 2-2 tie. UND's Darren Jensen records 23 saves, and Terry Kleisinger has 33 in the Wisconsin nets. The Sioux beat Northeastern University 6-2 in the semifinal, taking a 6-0 lead on goals by Glen White, Phil Sykes, Jim Archibald, Cary Eades, Troy Murray and Dusty Carroll. Jensen makes 24 stops, while Northeastern goalies make 26 stops.

Dec. 26, 1982 through Jan. 2, 1983: The Sioux make their first trip to Europe to play in the prestigious Spengler Cup tournament in Davos, Switzerland. UND registers a 1-4-1 record against older teams from the USSR, Czechoslovakia, Switzerland and West Germany.

March 16-17, March 22-23, 1984: The Sioux edge Rensselaer Polytechnic Institute in Troy, N.Y., 5-4 and 4-2, to advance to the NCAA semifinals in Lake Placid, N.Y., where they lose 2-1 in OT to the University of Minnesota-Duluth and edge Michigan State 6-5 in OT on a goal by wing Dean Barsness in the third-place game.

Jan. 11, 1986: In one of the most amazing comebacks in UND hockey history, the Sioux defeat Minnesota-Duluth 8-7 in OT in Duluth. UND trails 7-3 with 2:56 left in the third period before scoring four goals in 2:41 to force the OT. Scott Koberinski scores at 17:05, Brian Williams tallies twice at 17:58 and 19:10, and Chris Jensen ties it at 19:46. Ian Kidd's deflection of Glen Klotz's shot, only 50 seconds into OT, is the winner.

March 26-28, 1987: North Dakota wins its fifth NCAA crown and third in just nine years with Gasparini behind the bench. UND gets to the title game by virtue of a 5-2 victory over Harvard University in the semifinals in Joe Louis Arena in Detroit, Mich. Freshman Brent Bobyck, junior Bob Joyce, sophomore sensation Tony Hrkac, senior Mickey Krampotich and junior Steve Johnson score Sioux goals in the triumph over the Crimson, while freshman Ed Belfour makes 37 saves in goal. In the title game, UND takes a 3-0 first-period lead over Michigan State on goals by sophomore defenseman Ian Kidd, freshman Murray Baron and Joyce. The Spartans score midway through the second period before Sioux senior Malcolm Parks makes it 4-1. MSU cuts it to 4-2 at the end of two periods. Bobyck scores at 7:54, and MSU adds a late goal to make the final a 5-3 North Dakota decision. Belfour has only 15 saves in the tight-checking game played before 17,644 fans, a tournament record. Hrkac is named winner of the Hobey Baker Memorial Award as the top player in college hockey. John "Gino" Gasparini is named national coach of the year.

March 16-18, 1990: The Sioux travel to Boston for an NCAA tournament first-round series at Boston University where, after winning Game 1 by an 8-5 score, they drop two straight to the Terriers (5-3 and 5-0) and are eliminated from the tournament.

Nov. 27, 1992: Greg Johnson records his 169th assist to become UND's all-time assists leader as the Sioux defeat St. Cloud (Minn.) State 4-3 in Grand Forks.

Feb. 26, 1993: Greg Johnson assists on Brad Bombardir's goal at 19 seconds of the third period in a 5-1 win at Michigan Tech. The assist makes Johnson the WCHA's all-time assists leader and UND's all-time leading scorer. He also ties the WCHA record for career assists in league games when he assists on Marty Schriner's goal later in the period.

March 31 through April 2, 1993: Greg Johnson is named a first-team All-American for the second time in his career and finishes as runner-up to Maine's Paul Kariya in voting for the Hobey Baker

Memorial Award as college hockey's top player.

June 26, 1993: Incoming freshman Landon Wilson, son of former Sioux and UND Hall of Famer Rick Wilson, becomes UND's fifth first-round NHL draft choice when the Toronto Maple Leafs select him 19th overall.

April 9, 1994: John "Gino" Gasparini resigns as head coach of the Sioux hockey program after 16 years in that position. He leaves with three NCAA titles and a 392-248-24 record.

May 21, 1994: Dean Blais, a Sioux hockey assistant coach from 1980 to 1989, is named UND's 14th head hockey coach.

March 10-11, 1995: Under rookie head coach Dean Blais, the Sioux win their first playoff series in four years when they sweep host St. Cloud (Minn.) State 3-2 and 5-2 at the National Hockey Center. UND advances to the WCHA Final Five for the first time and drops a tight-checking, 3-2 decision to Minnesota.

1996 to 1997: The 1996-1997 season marks the 50th anniversary of Fighting Sioux hockey.

Feb. 21-22, 1997: The Fighting Sioux post back-to-back shutouts of Alaska Anchorage at Engelstad Arena to clinch the MacNaughton Cup as the WCHA's regular-season champions. North Dakota shares this honor with Minnesota.

March 14-15, 1997: The Sioux top Colorado College 5-1 in the semifinals of the WCHA Final Five to advance to the championship game against conference co-champion Minnesota. North Dakota

tops the Gophers 4-3 in overtime on a goal by Peter Armbrust to take home the Broadmoor Trophy as the WCHA playoff champions.

March 27-29, 1997: A 6-2 win over Cornell University in the NCAA West Regional tournament sends the Fighting Sioux to the NCAA Frozen Four for the first time in 10 years. In the semifinals in Milwaukee, Wis., the Sioux meet a familiar opponent in Colorado College. Goals by Jason Blake, Matt Henderson, Kevin Hoogsteen, Jesse Bull, David Hoogsteen and Adam Calder lift the Sioux to a 6-2 win over the Tigers and earn them their first trip to the NCAA title game in 10 years. In the championship game, Boston University jumps out to a 2-0 lead after the first period. The Sioux storm back in the second period, taking a 3-2 lead on goals by Curtis Murphy, David Hoogsteen and Matt Henderson. Boston ties it at 13:56, but a Henderson goal at 15:49 gives the Sioux the lead. David Hoogsteen's goal at 19:54 caps the Sioux's five-goal period. Boston scores a goal late in the third period to close the gap, but Adam Calder ices the victory with an empty-net goal. Freshman netminder Aaron Schweitzer turns away 25 Terrier shots. Henderson is the tournament Most Outstanding Player.

Feb. 27, 1998: The Sioux clinch their second-straight WCHA regular-season title with a 6-3 win over the University of Minnesota-Duluth.

March 28, 1998: The Fighting Sioux's season is cut short as the

University of Michigan defeats the Sioux 4-3 at the NCAA West Regional. The 30-8-1 season is the second-straight 30-plus win season and second-straight appearance in the NCAA tournament. Curtis Murphy, the WCHA's Player of the Year, is named a first-team All-American and a Hobey Baker Memorial Award finalist.

Feb. 20, 1999: History is made as the Sioux clinch their third-straight WCHA regular-season title with a 4-3 win over Alaska Anchorage. UND is just the second team in WCHA history to win three straight regular-season titles.

April 6, 2000: North Dakota makes its fourth trip to Providence, R.I., for the NCAA Frozen Four. North Dakota meets Maine in the semifinal and blanks the Black Bears 2-0. The final game finds UND against Boston College. Last season, Boston College knocks UND out of the playoffs in the quarterfinals. This time the Fighting Sioux prevail to win a 4-2 game for their seventh national title. Lee Goren is named to the NCAA all-tournament team and Most Outstanding Player.

April 7, 2001: The Sioux come within a whisker of becoming the first repeat national champions since Boston University in 1971 and 1972. But Boston College escapes with a 3-2 overtime victory on Krys Kolanos' goal. Earlier, the Sioux win UND's fourth MacNaughton Cup in five years. Jeff Panzer is a Hobey Baker Memorial Award finalist for the second-straight year.

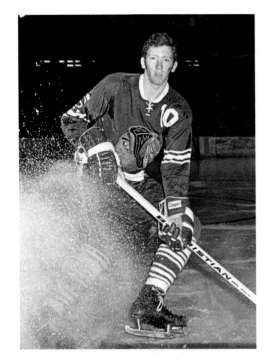

Top: Jim "Spook" Cahoon was a standout player on coach Rube Bjorkman's teams from 1969 to 1973. He led the Sioux in scoring as a junior and a senior. (photo, UND Athletics)

Bottom: Dixon Ward is the only UND player to finish with more than 100 goals and 100 assists. Ward shares ice time with, perhaps, some future UND players during the annual Skate with the Sioux. (photo, Eric Hylden, Grand Forks Herald)

Year	GP	W	L	T	Pct.	G	GA	P/PM
1929-30	2	1	1	0	.500	na	na	na
1930-31	1	0	1	0	.000	na	na	na
1932-33	9	1	8	0	.111	na	na	na
1935-36	4	2	2	0	.500	na	na	na
1936-46	No intercollegiate hockey					na	na	na
1946-47	13	7	6	0	.538	56	50	61/133
1947-48	16	11	5	0	.688	103	68	53/109
1948-49	22	9	12	1	.432	109	148	73/154
1949-50	23	15	6	2	.696	147	95	120/259
1950-51	26	12	12	2	.500	116	139	98/221
1951-52	25	13	11	1	.540	126	105	142/345
1952-53	20	15	5	0	.750	109	68	65/146
1953-54	27	14	12	1	.537	123	102	87/193
1954-55	28	14	13	1	.518	115	115	94/194
1955-56	28	11	16	1	.411	100	129	121/324
1956-57	29	18	11	0	.621	126	99	145/327
1957-58	32	24	7	1	.766	159	82	170/395
1958-59	31	20	10	1	.661	125	103	163/412
1959-60	32	19	11	2	.625	157	115	143/309
1960-61	29	9	19	1	.328	100	151	147/338
1961-62	26	9	17	0	.346	96	123	162/399
1962-63	32	22	7	3	.734	162	91	168/370
1963-64	25	12	11	2	.520	79	72	114/231
1964-65	33	25	8	0	.758	184	106	176/379
1965-66	30	17	12	1	.583	135	115	176/383
1966-67	29	19	10	0	.655	106	92	150/319
1967-68	33	20	10	3	.652	113	80	144/317
1968-69	29	18	10	1	.638	130	125	139/324
1969-70	30	14	15	1	.483	115	131	173/371
1970-71	33	14	17	2	.455	123	141	198/461
1971-72	36	21	14	1	.597	161	137	201/430
1972-73	36	17	17	2	.500	154	157	219/449
1973-74	34	10	23	1	.309	103	169	174/383
1974-75	36	6	28	2	.194	115	192	321/554
1975-76	36	15	21	0	.417	142	168	272/614
1976-77	38	19	19	0	.500	202	184	337/741
1977-78	38	15	22	1	.408	172	192	315/720
1978-79	42	30	11	1	.726	245	144	402/881
1979-80	40	31	8	1	.788	217	119	365/768
1980-81	38	21	15	2	.579	186	168	370/766
1981-82	47	35	12	0	.745	218	143	385/802
1982-83	36	21	13	2	.611	158	100	301/664
1983-84	45	31	12	2	.711	204	145	376/775
1984-85	42	24	16	2	.595	202	148	367/800
1985-86	41	24	16	1	.598	188	156	351/741
1986-87	48	*40	8	0	.833	264	129	422/888
1987-88	42	21	20	1	.512	174	160	366/779
1988-89	41	22	18	1	.549	164	138	372/787
1989-90	45	28	13	4	.667	252	175	432/978
1990-91	43	24	17	2	.581	207	171	373/863
1991-92	39	17	21	1	.449	170	199	472/1,086
1992-93	38	12	25	1	.329	138	173	374/873
1993-94	38	11	23	4	.342	119	164	417/1,015
1994-95	39	18	18	3	.500	151	169	371/914
1995-96	38	19	18	1	.513	162	155	323/708
1996-97	43	31	10	2	.744	190	130	301/719
1997-98	39	30	8	1	.782	188	115	366/786
1998-99	40	32	6	2	.813	199	104	323/772
1999-00	44	31	8	5	.761	192	97	301/703
2000-01	46	29	8	9	.728	183	121	321/686
Total	**1,905**	**1,070**	**753**	**82**	**.583**	**8,434**	**7,167**	**13,572/30,058**

Goals leader	Assists leader	Points leader
na	na	na
na	na	na
na	na	na
na	na	na
na	na	na
Bob Grina (13)	Bob Grina (8)	Bob Grina (21)
Bill Sullivan (18)	Gordon Christian (12)	Bill Sullivan, Gordon Christian (24)
Gordon Christian (25)	Jim Medved (22)	Jim Medved, Gordon Christian (41)
Milton "Prince" Johnson (35)	Buzz Johnson (23)	Prince Johnson, Buzz Johnson (50)
Ken Johannson (27)	Ken Johannson, George Dickinson (32)	Ken Johannson (59)
Ben Cherski (38)	Ken Johannson (30)	Ben Cherski (49)
Ben Cherski (30)	Ken Johannson (23)	Ben Cherski (44)
Ben Cherski (40)	Ken Purpur (31)	Ben Cherski (56)
Bill Reichart (33)	Mike Castellano (17)	Bill Reichart (45)
Bill Reichart (28)	Bill Reichart (23)	Bill Reichart (51)
Bill Reichart (36)	Jim Ridley (26)	Bill Reichart (60)
Jim Ridley, Art Miller (21)	Reg Morelli (26)	Jim Ridley (46)
Art Miller (24)	Art Miller (21)	Art Miller (45)
Reg Morelli (34)	Reg Morelli (31)	Reg Morelli (65)
Dave Merrifield (19)	Bill Colpitts (31)	Bill Colpitts (49)
Al McLean (19)	Al McLean (19)	Al McLean (38)
Dave Merrifield (21)	Al McLean (34)	Al McLean (53)
Gerry Kell (14)	Wayne Gurba, Terry Casey (12)	Gerry Kell (25)
Gerry Kell, Terry Casey (24)	Dennis Hextall (36)	Gerry Kell (55)
Terry Casey (26)	Dennis Hextall (29)	Terry Casey (54)
Bob Munro, Dave Kartio, Roger Bamburak (15)	Bob Lillo (18)	Bob Munro (30)
Dave Kartio (22)	Bob Munro (26)	Bob Munro (36)
Dave Kartio (21)	Bob Munro (30)	Bob Munro (43)
Earl Anderson (17)	Dave Bragnalo (21)	Dave Hudson (29)
Brian DePiero (18)	Brian DePiero (20)	Brian DePiero (38)
Jim Cahoon (24)	Jim Cahoon (31)	Jim Cahoon (55)
Larry Drader (19)	Jim Cahoon (36)	Jim Cahoon (52)
Brad Becker (13)	Alan Hangsleben, Brian DePiero (16)	Alan Hangsleben (25)
Bob DePiero (14)	Dave Geving (23)	Dave Geving (30)
Brad Becker (18)	Roger Lamoureux (26)	Roger Lamoureux (41)
Brad Becker (25)	Roger Lamoureux (40)	Roger Lamoureux (61)
Doug Smail (22)	Bill Himmelright (41)	Bill Himmelright (52)
Kevin Maxwell (31)	Mark Taylor (59)	Mark Taylor (83)
Doug Smail (43)	Mark Taylor (59)	Mark Taylor (92)
Troy Murray (33)	Troy Murray (45)	Troy Murray (78)
Phil Sykes (39)	Troy Murray (29)	Phil Sykes (63)
Dusty Carroll, Dave Donnelly (18)	James Patrick (36)	James Patrick (48)
Dan Brennan, Perry Berezan (28)	Dan Brennan (37)	Dan Brennan (65)
Jim Archibald (37)	Tony Hrkac (36)	Jim Archibald (61)
Bob Joyce (31)	Chris Jensen, Brian Williams (40)	Chris Jensen (65)
Bob Joyce (52)	Tony Hrkac (70)	Tony Hrkac (116)*
Steve Johnson (34)	Steve Johnson (51)	Steve Johnson (85)
Neil Eisenhut (22)	Lee Davidson (37)	Lee Davidson (53)
Russ Romaniuk (36)	Russ Parent (50)	Lee Davidson (75)
Russ Romaniuk (40)	Greg Johnson (61)	Greg Johnson (79)
Dixon Ward (33)	Greg Johnson (54)	Greg Johnson (74)
Kevin McKinnon (20)	Greg Johnson (45)	Greg Johnson (64)
Landon Wilson (18)	Marty Schriner, Nick Naumenko (22)	Landon Wilson, Mary Schriner (33)
Teeder Wynne (22)	Teeder Wynne (27)	Teeder Wynne (49)
Teeder Wynne (26)	Teeder Wynne (47)	Teeder Wynne (73)
David Hoogsteen (27)	Jason Blake (30)	David Hoogsteen (54)
Jason Blake (24)	Curtis Murphy (34)	Jason Blake (51)
Jason Blake (28)	Jason Blake (41)	Jason Blake (69)
Lee Goren (34)	Jeff Panzer (44)	Lee Goren, Jeff Panzer (63)
Bryan Lundbohm (32)	Jeff Panzer (55)	Jeff Panzer (81)

*NCAA record

Games played

1. Tony Hrkac (1986-87)	48
Bob Joyce (1986-87)	48
Steve Johnson (1986-87)	48
Scott Koberinski (1986-87)	48
Malcolm Parks (1986-87)	48

Goals scored

1. Bob Joyce (1986-87)	52
2. Tony Hrkac (1986-87)	46
3. Doug Smail (1979-80)	43
4. Ben Cherski (1953-54)	40
Russ Romaniuk (1990-91)	40

Power-play goals
(since 1975-76)

1. Doug Smail (1979-80)	17
2. Bob Joyce (1985-86)	16
Russ Romaniuk (1990-91)	16
4. Jim Archibald (1984-85)	15
Bob Joyce (1986-87)	15

Shorthanded goals
(since 1975-76)

1. Tony Hrkac (1986-87)	8
Doug Smail (1979-80)	8
3. Russ Romaniuk (1989-90)	6
4. Scott Dub (1987-88)	5
Gord Sherven (1981-82)	5
Frank Burggraf (1978-79)	5
Mike Burggraf (1978-79)	5
Dave Christian (1978-79)	5

Game-winning goals

1. Bob Joyce (1986-87)	8
Phil Sykes (1981-82)	8
Bryan Lundbohm (2000-01)	8

4. Lee Goren (1999-00)	7
Malcolm Parks (1986-87)	7
Jim Archibald (1983-84)	7
Mark Taylor (1978-79)	7

Assists

1. Tony Hrkac (1986-87)	70
2. Greg Johnson (1990-91)	61
3. Mark Taylor (1978-79)	59
Mark Taylor (1979-80)	59
5. Jeff Panzer (2000-01)	55

Points

1. Tony Hrkac (1986-87)	116
2. Mark Taylor (1979-80)	92
3. Bob Joyce (1986-87)	89
4. Doug Smail (1979-80)	87
5. Steve Johnson (1987-88)	85

Penalties

1. Jim Archibald (1984-85)	81
2. Jim Archibald (1983-84)	78
3. Mike Commodore (1998-99)	62
4. Landon Wilson (1993-94)	60
5. Mike Commodore (1999-00)	59
Marty Schriner (1992-93)	59

Penalty minutes

1. Jim Archibald (1984-85)	197
2. Jim Archibald (1983-84)	156
Marty Schriner (1992-93)	156
4. Mike Commodore (1999-00)	154
Mike Commodore (1998-99)	154

Games played (goalie)

1. Jon Casey (1983-84)	37
2. Toby Kvalevog (1995-96)	34

Ed Belfour (1986-87)	34
4. Peter Waselovich (1973-74)	33
5. Toby Kvalevog (1993-94)	32
Toby Kvalevog (1994-95)	32

Wins

1. Ed Belfour (1986-87)	29
2. Jon Casey (1983-84)	25
3. Karl Goehring (1997-98)	23
4. Karl Goehring (1998-99)	22
5. Peter Waselovich (1976-77)	21

Goals-against average

1. Karl Goehring (1999-00)	1.89
2. Mike Curran (1967-68)	2.14
3. Karl Goehring (1997-98)	2.27
4. Aaron Schweitzer (1996-97)	2.31
5. Ed Belfour (1986-87)	2.37

Save percentage

1. Karl Goehring (1999-00)	.927
2. Mike Curran (1967-68)	.919
3. Karl Goehring (2000-01)	.918
4. Ed Belfour (1986-87)	.915
Karl Goehring (1998-99)	.915

Shutouts

1. Karl Goehring (1999-00)	8
2. Aaron Schweitzer (1996-97)	4
Gerald "Spike" Schultz (1953-54)	4
4. Karl Goehring (2000-01)	3
Karl Goehring (1998-99)	3
Ed Belfour (1986-87)	3
Mike Curran (1967-68)	3

(photos, John Stennes, Grand Forks Herald)

Doug Smail

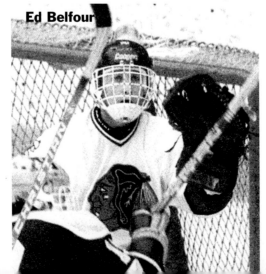

Ed Belfour

Mark Taylor

Games played
1.	Lee Davidson (1986-90)	167
2.	Jeff Panzer (1997-01)	164
3.	Jeff McLean (1987-88, 1989-92)	163
	Dixon Ward (1988-92)	163
5.	Russ Parent (1986-90)	162
	Brian Williams (1982-86)	162
	Mike Stone (1977-82)	162

Goals scored
1.	Ben Cherski (1951-55)	131
2.	Dixon Ward (1988-92)	110
3.	Bob Joyce (1984-87)	101
4.	Phil Sykes (1978-82)	98
5.	Bill Reichart (1954-57)	97
	Mark Taylor (1976-80)	97

Power-play goals
1.	Mark Taylor (1976-80)	43
2.	Dixon Ward (1988-92)	40
3.	Russ Romaniuk (1988-91)	33
4.	Bob Joyce (1984-87)	32
5.	Chris Jensen (1982-86)	29
	Doug Smail (1977-80)	29

Shorthanded goals
1.	Russ Romaniuk (1988-91)	12
2.	Scott Dub (1984-88)	10
3.	Tony Hrkac (1984-85, 86-87)	9
	Doug Smail (1977-80)	9
5.	Dusty Carroll (1979-83)	7
	Phil Sykes (1978-82)	7

Game-winning goals
1.	Mark Taylor (1976-80)	18
2.	Lee Goren (1997-00)	13
3.	Bob Joyce (1984-87)	12
	Jim Archibald (1981-85)	12
	Bryan Lundbohm (1998-01)	12

Assists
1.	Greg Johnson (1989-93)	198
2.	Mark Taylor (1976-80)	168
3.	Jeff Panzer (1997-01)	148
4.	Rick Zaparniuk (1976-80)	125
5.	Lee Davidson (1986-90)	122

Points
1.	Greg Johnson (1989-93)	272
2.	Mark Taylor (1976-80)	265
3.	Jeff Panzer (1997-01)	228
4.	Dixon Ward (1988-92)	219
5.	Lee Davidson (1986-90)	202

Penalties
1.	Jim Archibald (1981-85)	247
2.	Marty Schriner (1990-94)	192
3.	Mike Commodore (1997-00)	151
4.	Scott Marvin (1973-74, 75-78)	135
	Dean Dachyshyn (1979-83)	135

Penalty minutes
1.	Jim Archibald (1981-85)	540
2.	Marty Schriner (1990-94)	487
3.	Mike Commodore (1997-00)	382
4.	Scott Marvin (1973-74, 75-78)	297
5.	Dean Dachyshyn (1979-83)	289

Games played (goalie)
1.	Toby Kvalevog (1993-97)	121
2.	Karl Goehring (1997-01)	118
3.	Peter Waselovich (1973-77)	104
4.	Scott Brower (1984-88)	90
5.	Mike Curran (1965-68)	86

Wins
1.	Karl Goehring (1997-01)	80
2.	Toby Kvalevog (1993-97)	52
	Jon Casey (1980-84)	52
4.	Scott Brower (1984-88)	47
5.	Darren Jensen (1979-83)	46

Winning percentage
(minimum 40 games)
1.	Andy Kollar (1998-present)	.837
2.	Karl Goehring (1997-01)	.765
3.	Jon Casey (1980-84)	.701
4.	Bob Iwabuchi (1978-80)	.679
5.	Darren Jensen (1979-83)	.669

Goals-against average
(minimum 40 games)
1.	Karl Goehring (1997-2001)	2.23
2.	Bob Peabody (1957-59)	2.55
3.	Andy Kollar (1998-present)	2.71
4.	Joe Lech (1962-65)	2.82
5.	Mike Curran (1965-68)	2.92

Save percentage
(minimum 40 games)
1.	Karl Goehring (1997-2001)	.918
2.	Jon Casey (1980-84)	.910
3.	Andy Kollar (1998-present)	.904
4.	Mike Curran (1965-68)	.897
5.	Darren Jensen (1979-83)	.894

Shutouts
1.	Karl Goehring (1997-2001)	15
2.	Aaron Schweitzer (1996-98)	5
	Tom Yurkovich (1954-57)	5
	Gerald "Spike" Schultz (1953-55)	5
5.	Scott Brower (1984-88)	4
	Joe Lech (1962-65)	4

Top: Ben Cherski ranks as one of UND's great players. Cherski is No. 1 in career goals, with 131 in just 100 games. His career spanned from 1951 to 1954. (photo, UND Athletics)

Bottom: Greg Johnson finished his career as UND's all-time leading scorer — with 272 points in 155 games. (photo, Eric Hylden, Grand Forks Herald)

1946-47: None
1947-48: Game captains
1948-49: Bob Murray
1949-50: Jim Medved
1950-51: Bob Krumholz, Bob May
1951-52: Ken Johannson
1952-53: Ken Johannson
1953-54: None
1954-55: None
1955-56: None
1956-57: Mike Castellano, Bill Reichart
1957-58: Jim Ridley, Ed Willems
1958-59: Bill Steenson, Julian Brunetta, Joe Poole
1959-60: Guy LaFrance, Art Miller, Ed Thomlinson
1960-61: John Gray, Gerry Walford
1961-62: John Gray, Ernie Dyda, Curt Roseborough
1962-63: Maurice "Sonny" Roberge, George Goodacre, Dan Storsteen
1963-64: Maurice "Sonny" Roberge
1964-65: Don Ross, Gerry Kell, Dave Mazur

1965-66: Terry Casey, Roy Davidson, Dennis Hextall
1966-67: Dave Janaway, Jerry Lafond
1967-68: Mike Furlong, John Gasparini, Terry Ogden
1968-69: Bob Munro, Bob Tuff
1969-70: Dave Hudson, John Marks
1970-71: Mike Baumgartner, Brian DePiero
1971-72: Brian DePiero, Rick Wilson
1972-73: Earl Anderson, Jim Cahoon, Al Henry
1973-74: Larry Drader, Alan Hangsleben
1974-75: Daryl Drader, Larry Drader, Ken Gibb
1975-76: Bob DePiero, Daryl Drader, Scott Marvin
1976-77: Bob DePiero, Tom Goddard, Roger Lamoureux
1977-78: Scott Marvin, Mike Burggraf, Bill

Himmelright
1978-79: Mike Burggraf, Bill Himmelright, Mark Taylor
1979-80: Mark Taylor, Marc Chorney, Erwin Martens
1980-81: Marc Chorney, Paul Chadwick, Phil Sykes
1981-82: Cary Eades, Phil Sykes
1982-83: Dunstan Carroll, Dean Dachyshyn
1983-84: Dan Brennan, Bill Whitsitt, Rick Zombo
1984-85: Scott Sandelin, Jim Archibald
1985-86: Scott Sandelin, Brian Williams, Glen Klotz, Mickey Krampotich, Ian Kidd
1986-87: Bob Joyce, Mickey Krampotich, Ian Kidd
1987-88: Steve Johnson, Scott Dub, Tom Benson
1988-89: Grant Paranica, Scott Koberinski
1989-90: Lee Davidson, Russ Parent, Brent

Bobyck
1990-91: Dave Hakstol, Russ Romaniuk
1991-92: Dave Hakstol, Greg Johnson, Dane Jackson, Dixon Ward
1992-93: Greg Johnson, Brad Bombardir, Chris Gotziaman
1993-94: Brad Bombardir, Kevin McKinnon, Chris Gotziaman
1994-95: Keith Murphy, Scott Kirton, Kevin Rappana
1995-96: Dane Litke, Teeder Wynne, Nick Naumenko
1996-97: Dane Litke, Kevin Hoogsteen, Mark Pivetz
1997-98: Mitch Vig, Curtis Murphy, Matt Henderson
1998-99: Adam Calder, David Hoogsteen, Brad Williamson
1999-00: Peter Armbrust, Jason Ulmer, Lee Goren
2000-01: Jeff Panzer, Karl Goehring, Bryan Lundbohm

Dunstan "Dusty" Carroll played on national championship teams at UND in both 1980 and 1982. (photo, John Stennes, Grand Forks Herald)

Dave Hudson was one of the first Sioux players to break into professional hockey. Hudson played at UND from 1967 to 1970. (photo, University Relations)

All-Americans

First- and second-team members named by the American Hockey Coaches Association

1950-51:
John Noah, D (1st)
1951-52:
Ben Cherski, C (2nd)
1952-53:
Ben Cherski, C (1st)
1953-54:
Ben Cherski, C (1st) Spike Schultz, G (1st)
1954-55:
Bill Reichart, C (1st)
1955-56:
Bill Reichart, C (1st)
1956-57:
Bill Reichart, F (1st)
Bill Steenson, D (1st)
1957-58:
Bill Steenson, D (1st)
1959-60:
Reg Morelli, C (1st)
1962-63:
Don Ross, D (1st)
Al McLean, F (1st)
Dave Merrifield, F (1st)
1964-65:
Don Ross, D (1st)
1965-66:
Terry Casey, C (1st)
1966-67:
Jerry Lafond, D (1st)
1967-68:
Terry Abram, D (1st)
Bob Munro, C (1st)
1968-69:
Bob Munro, C (1st)
John Marks, D (1st)
1969-70:
John Marks, D (1st)
1971-72:
Alan Hangsleben, D (1st)
1978-79:
Bob Iwabuchi, G (1st)
Kevin Maxwell, C (1st)
1979-80:
Mark Taylor, C (1st)
Howard Walker, D (1st)
1980-81:
Marc Chorney, D (1st)
1982-83:
James Patrick, D (1st)
1983-84:
Jon Casey, G (1st)

1985-86:
Scott Sandelin, D (2nd)
1986-87:
Tony Hrkac, C (1st)
Bob Joyce, F (1st)
Ian Kidd, D (1st)
Ed Belfour, G (2nd)
1987-88:
Steve Johnson, C (1st)
1989-90:
Russ Parent, D (1st)
Lee Davidson, C (2nd)
1990-91:
Greg Johnson, C (1st)
1991-92:
Greg Johnson, C (2nd)
1992-93:
Greg Johnson, C (1st)
1995-96:
Teeder Wynne, F (2nd)
1996-97:
Curtis Murphy, D (2nd)
David Hoogsteen, F (2nd)
1997-98:
Curtis Murphy, D (1st)
Jason Blake, F (2nd)
Karl Goehring, G (2nd)
1998-99:
Jason Blake, C (1st)
Brad Williamson, D (1st)
Jay Panzer, F (2nd)
1999-00:
Karl Goehring, G (1st) Jeff Panzer, C (1st)
Lee Goren, F (2nd)
2000-01:
Jeff Panzer, C (1st)
Travis Roche, D (1st)
Bryan Lundbohm, F (2nd)

The Nationalists

1949: (Stockholm, Sweden)
Milton "Prince" Johnson
Russell "Buzz" Johnson
1950: (London, England)
Milton "Prince Johnson
Russell "Buzz" Johnson
1955: (four sites in Germany)
Gordon Christian
Dan McKinnon
1958: (Oslo, Norway)
Gordon Christian
Dan McKinnon
Coach Cal Marvin
1961: (Geneva, Switzerland)

Tom Yurkovich
1965: (Tampere, Finland)
Dan Storsteen
Manager Cal Marvin
1966: (Ljubjana, Yugoslavia)
Don Ross
1967: (Vienna, Austria)
Don Ross
Arthur Miller
Terry Casey
1969: (Stockholm, Sweden)
Bill Reichart
1970: (Bucharest, Romania)
Mike Curran
Don Ross
1971: (Geneva, Switzerland)
Don Ross
Mike Curran
1973: (Graz, Austria)
Earl Anderson
Alan Hangsleben
1974: (Ljubjana, Yugoslavia)
Alan Hangsleben
1976: (Katowice, Poland)
Mike Curran
1986: (Moscow, USSR)
Scott Sandelin
Brian Williams
1999: (Lillehammer, Norway)
Jason Blake
2000: (St. Petersburg, Russia)
Karl Goehring

The Olympians

1952: (Oslo, Norway)
John Noah
1956: (Cortina d'Ampezzo, Italy)
Gordon Christian,
Dan McKinnon,
Ken Purpur
1964: (Innsbruck, Austria)
Tom Yurkovich,
Bill Reichart
1968: (Grenoble, France)
Don Ross
1972: (Sapporo, Japan)
Mike Curran

John Noah of Crookston, Minn., was the first All-America player in UND history. Noah, a defenseman from 1947 to 1951, earned All-America honors in the 1950-1951 season. He also was UND's first Olympic player, playing in 1952. (photo courtesy of John Noah)

1980: (Lake Placid, N.Y.)
Dave Christian,
Kevin Maxwell
1984: (Sarajevo, Yugoslavia)
Dave Tippett,
James Patrick,
Dave Donnelly
1988: (Calgary, Alta.)
Bob Joyce,
Gord Sherven
1992: (Albertville, France)
Dave Tippett
1994: (Lillehammer, Norway)
Greg Johnson

World Juniors
United States
Craig Ludwig
Scott Sandelin
Steve Johnson
Ian Kidd
Lee Davidson
Chris Gotziaman
Marty Schriner
Toby Kvalevog
Landon Wilson
Canada
Troy Murray
James Patrick
Geoff Smith
Jason Herter
Greg Johnson
Brad Bombardir

Tournament appearances

25, Boston University, 1950-2000
25, Minnesota, 1953-2001
24, Michigan, 1948-2001
22, Boston College, 1948-2001
21, Michigan St. 1959-2001
18, Clarkson, 1957-1999
18, Wisconsin, 1970-2001
17, North Dakota, 1958-2001
16, Harvard, 1955-1994
15, St. Lawrence, 1952-2001
14, Denver, 1958-2000

Current consecutive tournament appearances

11, Michigan, 1991-2001
8, Michigan St., 1994-2001
5, North Dakota, 1997-2001
4, Boston College, 1998-2001
3, Maine, 1999-2001
3, St. Lawrence, 1999-2001

Tournament wins

39, Minnesota, 1953-2001
38, Michigan, 1948-2001
32, Boston U., 1950-2000
30, North Dakota, 1958-2001
28, Wisconsin, 1970-2001
24, Michigan St., 1959-2001
23, Boston College, 1948-2001
20, Lake Superior St., 1985-1996
20, Maine, 1987-2001
17, Denver, 1958-1999

NCAA championships

9, Michigan, 1948-1998
7, North Dakota, 1959-2000
5, Denver, 1958-1969
5, Wisconsin, 1973-1990
4, Boston U., 1971-1995
3, Michigan Tech, 1962-1975
3, Minnesota, 1974-1979
3, Lake Superior St., 1988-1994
2, Colorado College, 1950-1957

2, Cornell, 1967-1970
2, Rensselaer, 1954-1985
2, Michigan St., 1966-1986
2, Maine, 1993-1999
2, Boston College, 1948-2001

Frozen Four appearances

20, Boston U., 1950-1997
20, Michigan, 1948-2001
17, Boston College, 1948-2001
16, Minnesota, 1953-1995
14, North Dakota, 1958-2001
12, Harvard, 1955-1994
11, Denver, 1958-1986
10, Michigan Tech, 1956-1981
10, Michigan St., 1959-2001
9, Wisconsin, 1970-1990
9, Colorado College, 1948-1997
9, St. Lawrence, 1952-2000

Consecutive Frozen Four appearances

4, Boston College, 1998-2001
2, North Dakota, 2000-2001

Frozen Four wins

24, Michigan, 1948-2001
20, North Dakota, 1958-2001
18, Boston U., 1950-1997
15, Minnesota, 1953-1995
14, Denver, 1958-1986
13, Wisconsin, 1970-1990
11, Michigan Tech, 1956-1981
10, Boston College, 1948-2001
8, Michigan St., 1959-1999
7, Lake Superior St., 1988-1994
7, Cornell, 1967-1980
7, Colorado College, 1948-1997

NCAA All-Tournament Team (UND)

1958, Bill Steenson D
1959, Reg Morelli F; Ed Thomlinson F
1963, George Goodacre D; Don Ross D; Al McLean F; Dave Merrifield F; Don

Stokaluk F
1968, Terry Abram D; Bob Munro F
1979, Howard Walker D; Mark Taylor F
1980, Marc Chorney D; Doug Smail F; Phil Sykes F
1982, Darren Jensen G; James Patrick D; Cary Eades F; Phil Sykes F
1984, Dean Barsness F
1987, Ed Belfour G; Ian Kidd D; Tony Hrkac F; Bob Joyce F
1997, David Hoogsteen F; Matt Henderson F; Curtis Murphy D; Aaron Schweitzer G
2000. Lee Goren F; Bryan Lundbohm F; Mike Commodore D; Karl Goehring G
2001, Bryan Lundbohm F; Travis Roche D

NCAA Tournament Most Outstanding Players (UND)

Reg Morelli, 1959
Al McLean, 1963
Doug Smail, 1980
Phil Sykes, 1982
Tony Hrkac, 1987
Matt Henderson, 1997
Lee Goren, 2000

UND Hobey Baker Memorial Award finalists

James Patrick, 1983
Jon Casey, 1984
Scott Sandelin, 1986
Steve Johnson, 1988
Russ Parent, 1990
Greg Johnson, 1991, 1992, 1993
Jason Blake, 1997, 1999
Curtis Murphy, 1998
Jeff Panzer, 2000, 2001

Hobey Baker winner

Tony Hrkac, 1987

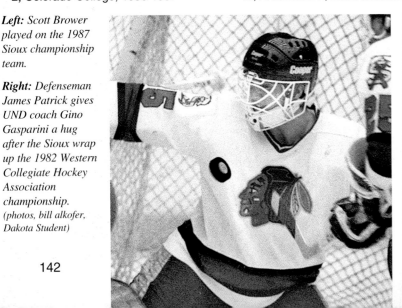

Left: Scott Brower played on the 1987 Sioux championship team.

Right: Defenseman James Patrick gives UND coach Gino Gasparini a hug after the Sioux wrap up the 1982 Western Collegiate Hockey Association championship. (photos, bill alkofer, Dakota Student)

WCHA Coach of the Year

1964-65	Bob Peters
1966-67	Bill Selman
1978-79	John "Gino" Gasparini
1981-82	John "Gino" Gasparini
1986-87	John "Gino" Gasparini
1996-97	Dean Blais
1998-99	Dean Blais
2000-01	Dean Blais

National Coach of the Year
(Spencer Penrose Award)

1986-87	John "Gino" Gasparini
1996-97	Dean Blais
2000-01	Dean Blais

Years	Coach	Overall	Record	League	Record
1929-32	Joe Brown	1-2-0	(.333)	na	na
1932-33	Noland Franz	1-8-0	(.111)	na	na
1935-36	Buck Cameron	2-2-0	(.500)	na	na
1936-46	Intramurals	na	na	na	na
1946-47	John Jamieson	7-6-0	(.538)	na	na
1947-49	Don Norman	20-17-1	(.539)	na	na
1949-56	Cliff "Fido" Purpur	94-75-8	(.554)	42-42-0	(.500)
1956-57	Al Renfrew	18-11-0	(.621)	13-9-0	(.591)
1957-59	Bob May	44-17-2	(.714)	21-5-1	(.796)
		14-7-0**	No league	35-21-1***	
1959-64	Barry Thorndycraft	71-65-8	(.521)	59-49-4	(.545)
1964-66	Bob Peters	42-20-1	(.674)	26-12-0	(.684)
1966-68	Bill Selman	39-20-3	(.653)	29-14-1	(.670)
1968-78	Rube Bjorkman	149-186-11	(.447)	121-162-7	(.429)
1978-94	Gino Gasparini	392-248-24	(.608)	277-197-21	(.581)
1994-present	Dean Blais	190-76-24	(.696)	131-58-19	(.675)

** Old WIHL disbanded after 1957-58 season.
***Old WIHL played interlocking schedules, these figures for games only vs. old WIHL members.

Barry Thorndycraft (left) coached the 1963 Fighting Sioux to the NCAA championship in his next-to-last season as coach during his five-year tenure from 1959 to 1964. Thorndycraft finished with an overall record of 71 wins, 65 losses and eight ties at UND. Thorndycraft's Sioux beat Denver University 6-5 in the 1963 NCAA title game. (photo, UND Special Collections)

It was only fitting that a Zamboni lead the funeral procession for North Dakota's only National Hockey League player — Cliff "Fido" Purpur of Grand Forks, N.D. — after his death in 2001. Purpur, who coached at every level of hockey in Grand Forks after he returned from pro hockey, was UND's hockey coach from 1949 through 1956. He compiled a 94-75-8 overall record and a 42-42 mark in league play. The city rink in Grand Forks is named in his honor. (photo, John Stennes, Grand Forks Herald)